The Data Librarian's Handbook

Every purchase of a Facet book helps to fund CILIP's
advocacy, awareness and accreditation programmes
for information professionals.

The Data Librarian's Handbook

Robin Rice and John Southall

© Robin Rice and John Southall 2016

Published by Facet Publishing
7 Ridgmount Street, London WC1E 7AE
www.facetpublishing.co.uk

Facet Publishing is wholly owned by CILIP: the Chartered Institute of Library and Information Professionals.

Robin Rice and John Southall have asserted their right under the Copyright, Designs and Patents Act 1988 to be identified as authors of this work.

Except as otherwise permitted under the Copyright, Designs and Patents Act 1988 this publication may only be reproduced, stored or transmitted in any form or by any means, with the prior permission of the publisher, or, in the case of reprographic reproduction, in accordance with the terms of a licence issued by The Copyright Licensing Agency. Enquiries concerning reproduction outside those terms should be sent to Facet Publishing, 7 Ridgmount Street, London WC1E 7AE.

Every effort has been made to contact the holders of copyright material reproduced in this text, and thanks are due to them for permission to reproduce the material indicated. If there are any queries please contact the publisher.

British Library Cataloguing in Publication Data
A catalogue record for this book is available from the British Library.

ISBN 978-1-78330-047-1 (paperback)
ISBN 978-1-78330-098-3 (hardback)
ISBN 978-1-78330-183-6 (e-book)

First published 2016

Text printed on FSC accredited material.

Typeset from authors' files in 10/13 pt Palatino Linotype and Open Sans by Facet Publishing Production.
Printed and made in Great Britain by CPI Group (UK) Ltd, Croydon, CR0 4YY.

Contents

Acknowledgements ix

Preface xi

1 Data librarianship: responding to research innovation..............1
    The rise of data librarians..1
    Addressing early demand for data services in the social sciences.................3
    The growth of data collections..8
    The origins of data libraries..10
    A new map of support for services and researchers 15

2 What is different about data? 19
    Attitudes and pre-conceptions 19
    Is there a difference if data are created or re-used? 22
    Data and intellectual property rights..23
    The relationship of metadata to data 24
    Big data 27
    Long tail data 28
    The need for data citation 29
    Embracing and advocating data curation.......................................31

3 Supporting data literacy 35
    Information literacy with data awareness......................................35
    Categories of data 41
    Top tips for the reference interview 42
    What has statistical literacy got to do with it? 44
    Data journalism and data visualization 45
    Topics in research data management...46
    Training in data handling..50

4 Building a data collection 53
Policy and data..53
Promoting and sustaining use of a collection.................................58
Embedding data within the library..64

5 Research data management service and policy: working across your institution..67
Librarians and RDM..67
Why does an institution need an RDM policy? 69
What comprises a good RDM policy? 73
Tips for getting an RDM policy passed...73
Toolkits for measuring institutional preparedness for RDM..........74
Planning RDM services: what do they look like? 76
Evaluation and benchmarking 81
What is the library's role? 83

6 Data management plans as a calling card.................................87
Responding to challenges in data support.....................................87
Leading by example: eight vignettes..87
  Social science research at the London School of Economics and Political Science..88
  Clinical medical research at the London School of Hygiene and Tropical Medicine...89
  Archaeological research at the University of California, Los Angeles 91
  Geological research at the University of Oregon.........................93
  Medical and veterinary research at the University of Glasgow 95
  Astronomical research at Columbia University 96
  Engineering research at the University of Guelph.......................97
  Health-related social science research at the University of Bath 99
The snowball effect of data management plans 101

7 Essentials of data repositories..103
Repository versus archive? 103
Put, get, search: what is a repository? 104
Scoping your data repository..106
Choosing a metadata schema 108
Managing access 111
Data quality review (or be kind to your end-users) 112
Digital preservation planning across space and time..................114
Trusted digital repositories 116
The need for interoperability..117

8 Dealing with sensitive data 121
Challenging assumptions about data...121
Understanding how researchers view their research..................122
Sensitivity and confidentiality – a general or specific problem? 124
A role in giving advice on consent agreements 126
Storing and preserving confidential data effectively 128

9 Data sharing in the disciplines **137**
Culture change in academia 137
   In the social sciences.. 138
   In the sciences 139
   In the arts and humanities 143

10 Supporting open scholarship and open science **147**
Going green: impact of the open access movement 147
Free software, open data and data licences 149
Big data as a new paradigm? 150
Data as first-class research objects... 152
Reproducibility in science... 153
Do libraries need a reboot? 156

References **161**

Index **169**

Acknowledgements

We would first like to thank our spouses and our bosses for offering us their support and especially patience as we wrote this book without our work and private lives slowing down. Helen Carley, our publisher, always showed faith in us, even when we worried that the field of data librarianship was changing faster than we could even fix our knowledge onto the page. Laine Ruus read and critiqued our early drafts, debated with us about some of our assumptions, and added a fresh perspective. Members of the International Association for Social Science Information Service and Technology (IASSIST), our main professional society, have helped us crystalize our knowledge about data librarianship throughout our careers, and provided a supportive and fun community allowing us to thrive in our work.

Robin Rice and John Southall

Preface

This is not the first book written about data librarianship, and hopefully it will not be the last, but it is one of very few, all written within the past few years, that reflects the growing interest in research data support. Academic data librarians help staff and students with all aspects of this peculiar class of digital information – its use, preservation and curation, and how to support researchers' production and consumption of it in ever greater volumes, to create new knowledge.

Our aim is to offer an insider's view of data librarianship as it is today, with plenty of practical examples and advice. At times we try to link this to wider academic research agendas and scholarly communication trends past, present and future, while grounding these thoughts back in the everyday work of data librarians and other information professionals.

We would like to tell you a little bit about ourselves as the authors, but first a word about you. We have two primary groups of readers in mind for this book: library and iSchool students and their teachers, and working professionals (especially librarians) learning to deal with data. We would be honoured to have this book used as an educational resource in library and information graduate programmes, because we believe the future of data librarianship (regardless of its origins, examined in Chapter 1) lies with academic libraries, and for that to become a stronger reality it needs to be studied as a professional and academic subject. To aid the use of this book as a text for study we have provided 'key take-away points' and 'reflective questions' at the end of each chapter. These can be used by teachers for individual or group assignments, or by individuals to self-assess and reinforce what they may have learned from reading each chapter.

Equally important, we empathetically address the librarian, academic, or other working expert who feels their working life is pulling them towards data support or that area of academic activity known as research data management (RDM). We appreciate that this subset of readers will bring many pre-existing abilities and knowledge to this area, so we attempt to fill in the missing portions as pragmatically as we can, while linking daily tasks to broader goals and progressive initiatives, some of which you will be well familiar with and others less so, depending on your area of expertise. As will become apparent in Chapter 1, virtually everyone working as data librarians today received no special training beyond learning on the job, professional development opportunities and, if we were lucky, some personal mentoring.

We hope that by foregrounding these groups we have closed a significant gap in this nascent body of literature. We have also considered the requirements of other potential readers, be they library managers hoping to create new data librarian posts, policy-makers in libraries and academia developing strategies for research data, or academic librarians and other support professionals compelled to add data support to an existing workload who could use a primer on the subject.

Although between us we have over 20 years of experience as data librarians we still find it tricky to describe our work (at the proverbial cocktail party). In that sense, writing this book has been a welcome opportunity to explore our own professional activities and proclivities, to compare and contrast with each other and with other data librarians and data professionals, and to draw out what is consistent, lasting and of most value in what we offer to the research communities we serve. Typically for data librarians, as we shall see, one of us comes from a library background, the other from research (sociology), and while we are both UK-based, one of us began our data librarian career in the USA (at the University of Wisconsin-Madison), so we aim for a cross-Atlantic view. Although we aim to provide a single voice to the book it has certainly been the case, given the variety of approaches to data support by both institutions and individual data librarians, that 'two heads are better than one' for this endeavour.

A few of our conventions are worth mentioning here. It is our intention to always use the word data in the plural form. Some uses in the singular may slip through, as it does in general culture, but we find that you can get used to using the term 'properly' if you try. Figure 0.1 sums up the situation well.

Figure 0.1 *Data: singular or plural?*
© XKCD Comics, 'Data'. Used in accordance with https://xkcd.com/license.html.

Where we cite literature, and especially the more seminal literature that has grown up in our field, we provide complete references at the end of the book in the time-honoured manner. However, as our working world is very much one that is always online, web-based resources are sprinkled throughout the book, not in separate footnotes, but embedded in the text, so that you may have a look and a play as you are reading. The fact that some of these URLs are bound to disappear over time is one we regretfully accept, but we hope there is enough context given for the reader to find either the resource discussed or a newer, equivalent tool for the job.

Some of the terminology we use may be unfamiliar to you. We find that much of it is authoritatively explained in the community resource called Open Research Glossary (www.righttoresearch.org/resources/OpenResearchGlossary), which we encourage you to use as a companion to the book. A note on referring to library patrons, which in itself can be revealing of different traditions and presumptions: some institutions use established terms such as 'reader'; some libraries or archival services developed specifically to support work with data refer to their main audience as 'users'. This will be discussed further in Chapter 1, but in our opinion both reader and user are acceptable terms, since one refers to the relationship of the researcher to a library-based support service and the other to their relationship with the data.

A final point, we are grateful that Facet Publishing have their own reasons for believing in a book on this topic at this time, and we very much welcome your interest as readers in data librarianship – a term we embrace that seems to encompass both the very new and the traditional in libraries – and hope that you find at least the beginnings of what you are seeking, and wish you well on your data journey or career.

Robin Rice and John Southall

CHAPTER 1
Data librarianship: responding to research innovation

The rise of data librarians

A university has been defined as 'just a group of buildings gathered around a library' (https://en.wikiquote.org/wiki/Shelby_Foote); in any case, the role of the library in academic life is a central one. Those working within libraries make a valuable contribution to supporting research and teaching as well as shaping the character and intellectual life of individual institutions. Whether a university focuses on the humanities, physical sciences, classics or any other number of disciplines, the librarian ultimately works to support learning and the spread of knowledge. This may take many established forms but increasingly there is a need to support new forms of information. Digital data is one particular new form. In the case of data collections and research data creation this has also led to the rise of a new kind of library professional: the data librarian. But to what extent is this in fact a new role and in what ways does it differ from traditional librarianship?

For example, one role of the librarian is to deal with what may be called the lifecycle of information resources. These are the varied tasks to do with evaluation, selection, purchasing and promotion, and preservation of materials within the library. This relies on having a good working knowledge of what readers in a particular area need for their work. It also draws on a familiarity with what is being made available by publishers and other suppliers of information resources. The terms employed to describe a researcher also indicate the orientation or origin of research support services. Some may prefer traditional terms such as patron or – as favoured at the University of Oxford – reader, since this gives continuity to existing provision. The medium or methodologies being applied to the data are unimportant. On the other hand those working on support services created specifically to deal with digital data may feel older terms are inappropriate or anachronistic. Since digital information is often used in conjunction with software it is no longer 'human-readable' at all and its value lies in the fact it can be easily supplied to researchers. Their role is to manipulate, interpret, analyse, watch, listen to, or more generally 'use' the data. For this reason data centres or repositories often refer to 'users' of data. Finally, a sense of what characterizes a particular library is also important in how these different elements relate to each other. This often forms the basis of collections development policy.

Traditional – that is to say established – library activity also covers developing procedures and materials that help make collection items discoverable and accessible. Cataloguing and organizing of materials is an ongoing area of work that forms a foundation of much of librarianship. Preservation and curation is another key responsibility – especially when access has to be maintained for material that is harder to find or no longer in print. Reference and user services are a common feature in most libraries that build on maintaining collections. Consultancy and training workshops that seek to support readers in analysing problems, framing research questions and working with information resources in a meaningful way are as well. Librarianship then begins to be understood not simply as something that supports discovery of and access to published titles or information resources but also as something that engages with the *conduct* of research and academic enquiry.

These are ways that librarians are responding to the needs of the university as well as to the specific intellectual needs of readers. However, new areas of activity are emerging that reflect changes in the research environment or expectations of the kind of support library professionals should offer. These are not necessarily new in themselves – and may have been undertaken by other sections of an institution's infrastructure to some extent. Issues to do with licensing of research materials are a common example. Another is giving advice on sources of funding and completing funding applications, reference management software, statistical analysis software and Computer Assisted Qualitative Data Analysis Software packages. Working with readers to access, manipulate or share research data is a way to demonstrate libraries' responsiveness to academic needs.

In the past these areas of activity have often been seen as administrative or technical stages of research that need to be dealt with but that are unrelated to traditional librarianship. In a seminal article on cyberinfrastructure, data and libraries in *D-Lib Magazine* Anna Gold has characterized these areas that fall outside the usual comfort zone of academic librarians as 'working upstream' in the research process, before the point of publication (Gold, 2007). Working upstream means not only working with information that has not yet been published, but understanding the processes by which various types of data are used to generate information. The rest of this chapter will show how research data have become an archived resource over the last 40 years or so, and how this is becoming normalized as just another information resource.

It will also show how research data are no longer the specialist reserve of IT departments but are indeed now part of the remit of academic libraries.

Addressing early demand for data services in the social sciences

The origins of data libraries and data archives in the 1960s and 1970s owe as much to the way that the social sciences were developing as an empirical research domain as they do to the rise of centralized computing in research.

The social science disciplines (politics, economics, psychology, sociology, anthropology, etc.) are generally thought of as softer than the physical or hard sciences, in part because of their methodologies – which at times may be more like an art than a science – and in part because their subject matter – humans and their behaviours, individually or collectively – are so hard to pin down or predict. The rigorous application of the scientific method towards the social sciences resulted in the rise of quantitative methods – statistics applied to samples of populations in order to describe, explain and predict behaviours. New computer processing techniques combined with quantitative methods gave social scientists much power to view social phenomena in an objective or scientific light, using measures such as psychological experiments, social surveys and economic indicators.

With the power of hindsight it is easy to see why, in the second half of the 20th century, there was a backlash of sorts by many social researchers against 'positivism', or a tendency to explain or reduce all human behaviour to statistical trends (Williams, Hodgkinson and Payne, 2004). In the UK the social sciences are still recovering from the effects of this backlash against quantitative methods, to the point that the primary funder of social science research, the Economic and Social Research Council (ESRC), has declared there is a dearth of quantitative skills and has been investing in a number of programmes to beef up the statistical literacy and numeric skills of researchers and students (Jones and Goldring, 2015). As with librarians, many of the students entering the social sciences do not think of themselves as 'numbers people' and gravitate more naturally towards qualitative methods (such as interviewing), the findings of which may be quite rich but involve sample selections and sizes that can seldom be generalized to a population.

Happily, these days the social sciences have moved beyond the 'quantitative–qualitative divide' of the last century and most social scientists believe that both methodological approaches are valid and even symbiotic (Brannen, 2005). For example a mixed methods approach generally turns to quantitative methods for discovering *how* people behave, and a qualitative approach is embraced for uncovering reasons *why*, especially when that is less well known. Or, if one is starting with collecting qualitative data, one might wish to compare the characteristics of the selected subjects against a reference population, using quantitative sources as benchmarks for contextualizing qualitative studies.

Then as now, social scientists are likely to turn towards secondary sources when they require quantitative datasets (consisting of one or more numeric data files, which may be encoded within software such as a spreadsheet, along with descriptive documentation about its contents). The use of data sources by the UK Data Archive (UKDA) roughly follows Pareto's 80/20 rule: 20% of resources are used by 80% of users, with 80% of datasets rarely if ever consulted, according to a previous director of the UKDA. (The Pareto distribution will be revisited in Chapter 4.) More often than not the highly used datasets are the well known national surveys and population census collections. Such resources have the advantage of being rich in variables (e.g. survey questions asked) so that new research questions can be interrogated, as well as having large, nationally representative samples. This is important for being able to study a sub-population (such as an ethnic minority group) and still have the statistical power to obtain useful, generalizable results. With a few exceptions (such as the British Election Study), it is government agencies which have the funding to carry out such extensive surveys and censuses, and not academic departments, let alone individual researchers. Another reason to share data about human subjects is to lower the response burden of individuals. Targeted commercial marketing has helped to create an atmosphere in which telephone and postal surveys are held in contempt by the intended subjects, lowering response rates across the board.

In this sense the social sciences, as the poor cousin of the more well endowed physical sciences, were the first disciplinary group to embrace data sharing and the re-use of data for reasons of economy or efficiency. However data about human subjects, like other observational data such as weather conditions, can never be replicated in the same circumstances – another strong rationale for sharing.

The earliest data libraries and archives – an American chronology

No one is better placed to recall the origins of academic data libraries in North America than Judith Rowe, retired Senior Data Services Specialist of Princeton University. In her entertaining speech at IASSIST's 25th anniversary conference banquet in Toronto on 20 May 1999, 'The Decades of My Life', she reminisced about the chronological developments in social science data collection and methods that she had witnessed (Rowe, 1999).

Rowe began her story as far back as the 1930s with the computing ideas of Alan Turing and Vannevar Bush and the existence of punch-card machines, but also the beginning of large-scale sampling, the Gallup Polls and the Brookings Institution. In addition to the massive global upheaval taking place in the 1940s, the World Bank, International Monetary Fund and the United Nations were founded; scaling and multivariate analytic techniques were developed; and 'Immediately after the [US] election in which the pollsters [incorrectly] chose Dewey over Truman the [US] Social Science Research Council appointed a committee . . . to find out why' (Rowe, 1999).

In the 1950s IBM produced its first 'real' computer, programming languages COBOL (common business-oriented language) and Fortran were invented, the Institute of Social Research at Michigan and the Bureau of Applied Social Research at Columbia was producing survey data galore, and the Roper Center had archived over 3000 surveys from 70 countries. But sampling and survey data were not yet mainstream: 'Walter Cronkite used UNIVAC 2 to predict the 1952 election. Unable to believe the computer report of such a complete Eisenhower sweep, he failed to report it' (Rowe, 1999). There was an echo of this in the 2012 US presidential elections, in which pundits derided statistician Nate Silver's probability-based predictions before he correctly predicted the presidential race outcomes in every state plus the District of Columbia – and thus the re-election of President Obama. This was characterized on the internet as a triumph for big data. (See, for example, Triumph of the Nerds: Nate Silver wins in 50 States, http://mashable.com/2012/11/07/nate-silver-wins.)

By the 1960s batch processing with punch cards was common, statistical packages SPSS (a social sciences package), SAS (a statistical analysis system) and plenty of others were being invented and developed at universities, and 'local data services were in place at Princeton, Northwestern, at the Universities of British Columbia and North Carolina as well as at Wisconsin and Yale' (Rowe, 1999). The Inter-university Consortium for Social Research at Michigan (later to have a P for Political added to become ICPSR) was founded as a consortium of eight institutions; the Library paid the membership fee on behalf of Princeton. The Council of Social Science Data Archives was funded by the National Science Foundation, and cross-Atlantic meetings about data archiving began. The ASCII standard was established and the Unix operating system was invented (Rowe, 1999).

A data archiving profession was in place by the 1970s and the pace was clearly accelerating. IASSIST was organized at a meeting sponsored by the World Congress of Sociology in Toronto in 1974 and met in London, Edinburgh, Cocoa Beach, Toronto, Itasca, Uppsala and Ottawa. 'The U.S. Census released off-the-shelf data products, both aggregate and [microdata] sample data, and significantly there was a growing involvement of traditional libraries in providing data services. The American Library Association constituted a subcommittee to recommend rules for cataloguing machine-readable data files' (Rowe, 1999).

Canada and the Data Liberation Initiative

Research institutions in Canada, such as the Universities of British Columbia, York University, Western Ontario and Carlton University, were also fostering data libraries and data support services in the social sciences in the same decades. However Canada has long suffered from a lack of national data archiving infrastructure. No central data archive, whether government-funded or consortium-based, has ever been established.

Statistics Canada, the national statistical service, for many years had a liberal policy of making aggregate data, microdata and other types of administrative data (postal codes, geocoded files, etc.) readily available and affordable. However, with a Conservative government in the mid-1980s that policy changed radically and all types of data became very expensive, and in the case of microdata more and more restricted from the mid-1990s.

Nevertheless the Canadian presence in IASSIST has always been a strong one (apparently sometimes known as Can-IASSIST), and its members eventually fostered the Data Liberation Initiative (DLI) beginning in the mid-1990s to pressure Statistics Canada to increase the amount of data released as public use microdata files and to reduce steep pricing regimes for 'special' data files or microdata (Boyko and Watkins, 2011). The movement was fairly successful; there is now a DLI section on the Statistics Canada website listing DLI products and members (www.statcan.gc.ca/eng/dli/dli). DLI is defined as 'a partnership between post secondary institutions and Statistics Canada for improving access to Canadian data resources'. DLI's early lobbying for more affordable pricing and release to the academic sector of all standard products was achieved, but critically microdata have largely fallen out of the standard products categories, and are now mainly available in secure data facilities only.

European data archives take shape

Meanwhile, in Europe there was a different trend than in North America: this was for centralized rather than localized social science data archives to be established as the result of encouragement and investment by funding bodies. In the social sciences there was an interest in preserving the data that were being generated by research into voting behaviour, for example (a former director of ICPSR singles out the efforts of two European political scientists – Stein Rokkan and Erwin K. Scheuch (Rockwell, 2001). There was also an appreciation of the slow but steady accumulation of government-sponsored survey data.

In 1976, the Council of European Social Science Data Archives (CESSDA) was founded – then a loosely tied federation of national data archives, which co-operated with each other in resource discovery through a shared catalogue, as well as training and procedures (see map, Figure 1.1). More recently it has received European Commission funding to establish common governance and closer co-ordination of activity. In 2013, a new consortium also called CESSDA was established as a permanent legal entity owned and financed by the individual member states' ministry of research or a delegated institution, hosted in Bergen, Norway; for more information see www.cessda.net/eng/About-us/History.

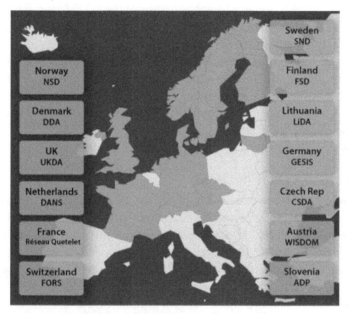

Figure 1.1 *Map of the Council of European Social Science Data Archives, CESSDA (2015)*

© *CESSDA, 2015. Used with permission.*
See www.cessda.net for the 15 current members and locations.

In Britain the establishment of the SSRC Data Bank (named after the Social Science Research Council but now known as the UKDA) occurred as early as 1967. In due course this held major surveys such as the British Household Panel Survey, the National Diet and Nutrition Survey, the British Crime Survey and the UK contribution to the European Social Survey.

Funding a data archive was seen by the research council as a way of ensuring social science data produced in the UK would be managed in the UK, rather than archived in data centres of foreign universities. It joined other emerging data archives such as the Central Archive for Empirical Social Research in (West) Germany (now part of GESIS [Gesellschaft Sozialwissenschaftlicher Infrastruktureinrichtungen] – Leibniz Institute for the Social Sciences) and the Norwegian Social Science Data Archive. The separation of those creating the original datasets from those who wished to preserve them was seen as an innovation. Initially these niche research sources were open mainly to those with the computing infrastructure and technical knowledge to use punch cards (later magnetic tape on reels), mainframe computers, and the ability to use programming languages to process and analyse the data.

Funding bodies and those working to preserve the data could see the value in encouraging broader use but technology was still a major brake to dissemination. Ivor Crewe, a former director of the UKDA, recalled, 'On my first day as Director of the Data Archive in October 1974 I asked to see a list of the Archive's users and was handed a tiny collection of address cards, no more than 20 in all. "No, not for last month, but since the Archive began." "That is the total since the Archive began" (was the reply).' The latter quotation is from one of several 'Memories of UKDA' from the 2007 anniversary event page (http://ukda40.data-archive.ac.uk/news/events.asp – refresh the page to view all quotes).

The growth of data collections

Expansion of these archives throughout the 1980s saw an increase in the amount of material being preserved at archives in North America and Europe. In the case of the UKDA, 450 datasets had been archived by 1975 and this had climbed to 6000 by 2007 (http://ukda40.data-archive.ac.uk/about/timeline.asp). In addition to direct deposits from government departments of annually collected survey data there was also a strong flow into the archives of data from academic research projects. This was new for the UKDA. Overall the variety and type of research data were therefore also increasing, but surveys were the mainstay of social science quantitative research – and still are. Consolidation led to a growing need to deal with the technical issues of data preservation simply in order to ensure the data remained physically readable by the tools available – let alone usable in the fullest sense of the word. Using machine-readable data (or digital data, as we say now) involved specialized knowledge of how to work with computer programs and make sense of codebooks and supporting documentation. In fact actually working with the storage media that was commonly used, such as punch cards, magnetic tape and so on, involved stages of data preparation and assistance from computer specialists. This kept control of datasets within data archives or the domain of computing centres.

Collections were taking shape as the number of deposits increased. Questions about how such collections could be promoted so that researchers would be aware of them became ever more important. These collections needed to be catalogued and documented effectively, and to support them expertise was drawn from the library sector. European archives tended to remain separate from academic libraries – physically and organizationally. But they valued the traditional skills librarians could bring to dealing with tasks of resource discovery and creating contextualizing documentation. In the 1980s, Bridget Winstanley, who joined the staff of the UKDA and Laine Ruus, who was recruited to the Swedish Social Science Data Archive, were the first librarians to work in European data archives.

In the USA datasets were held but not integrated at the discovery level into main libraries so another librarian, Sue Dodd, spearheaded a movement for including social science datasets into library catalogues to aid discovery by researchers. Her work resulted in a new chapter on machine-readable data files in the second edition of the authoritative *Anglo-American Cataloging Rules* (AACR II) published in 1978 (Gray, 2014). In 1982 the American Library Association published Dodd's manual *Cataloging Machine-Readable Data Files: an interpretive manual* (Dodd, 1982) and subsequently chose it as their prize book of the year. Data librarians and archivists collaborating in the IASSIST Classification Action Group 'tested the manual's guidelines, using them to prepare descriptions of their holdings. This was the necessary first step towards the long-sought goal of a union catalog for data files' (Adams, 2006, 11).

Delivery gives way to access

The technological brake that impeded the sharing and dissemination of datasets was slowly released with the expansion of online communications and the increasing capacity in academia for dealing with digital media in the late 1980s and 1990s. Meanwhile, mechanisms for delivery of data grew more and more sophisticated. Instead of punch cards, media such as, tape, drives and optical discs of one sort or another were used to both store and transport files. Some of these formats are now obsolete and some continue to be used today.

Delivery by post was a common method of transporting files and to do so the user had first to write to the archive (or have the site representative do so) requesting a particular dataset from a printed catalogue or inventory list. Then the magnetic tape or CD-ROM was mailed to the user, who would deliver it to the computing centre to be mounted and read. Floppy discs were often too small to hold large survey datasets, but CD-ROMs and DVDs could at least be read on the user's own desktop PC. Nevertheless the entire process of ordering and receiving data revolved around a physical delivery of media and usually took several weeks.

While pre-web internet systems helped facilitate faster access (e-mail, gopher, ftp), it was really the appearance of the world wide web, its html protocol and client-based browsers such as Mosaic in 1994/5 that has made it much more effective not only to deliver data to users, but also to deal with data collection descriptions, cataloguing, discovery and researcher support.

It is worth remembering that none of these advances would be possible without three underlying technological phenomena. First, the steadily increasing capacity of online storage allows greater volumes of data to be held on spinning disc drives as opposed to slower offline storage such as tape or CD-ROMs. Considering that the cost per byte of storage media has dropped exponentially for three decades, it is little wonder so much has been achieved in the same period and the pace of this has been discussed as part of Kryder's Law. Second, improvements in computing processing speeds (central processing units) and memory (cached storage) of computers themselves have increased the speed at which files can be copied, making copying almost instantaneous for all but the largest of files. Enter Moore's Law, which predicts that the processing speed of computing doubles every two years. Eventually personal computers – building on the invention of the microchip, user interface enhancements such as the mouse pioneered by Apple, and software simplifications such as those developed by Microsoft – took the place of large, centralized mainframe computers to which computing jobs were submitted through 'dumb terminals' to be run in batch mode while the researcher waited for the result – often overnight. Third, the telecommunications industry ensured that, as the internet became a viable means of delivering online services for profit, bandwidth increased again and again, with high throughput fibre-optic cables replacing wire to provide the backbone of a highly resilient global network.

All these developments have combined to move user expectations away from the idea of awaiting a *delivery* of data. They now look for support as readers in a library context where the emphasis is not simply on discovering information resources but also on the new concept of *access*. Expectations now are for an almost seamless ability to search, find and then use research data in one's studies immediately.

The origins of data libraries

It would be a mistake to think all these developments have been smooth and of the same kind. There have been different models of how to create and disseminate data collections to academia and knowledge of this can usefully illustrate how services may be set up or managed for those new to this field. As noted, in Western Europe the dominant trend was to found centralized data services sponsored by national research councils. In North America the initial trend was towards smaller initiatives based in computing centres or academic departments. For example to ensure local support for data-intensive social science research, a number of research institutions in North America set up local data archives or libraries to manage and provide access to data collections and to manage requests from national data and statistical organizations. Depending on the era the service was established, hemisphere, local environment and available talent, these services took a number of different shapes (see Table 1.1). Significant cuts in funding during the recession of the 1990s had a further impact on this evolution. Some European data centres closed and North American services increasingly moved into academic library settings where budgets were more stable.

Table 1.1 *The earliest social science data libraries, centres and archives*
Source: http://goo.gl/gQJrK8, reprinted with permission of Luis Martinez.
Several social science data archives, centres and libraries were in place by the 1970s, and many more were established by the end of the 20th century.

Institution	Year	Type	Country	Other names
Roper Center	1957	Data centre	USA	
Berkeley	1958	Data library/service	USA	
GESIS – Leibniz Institute for the Social Sciences	1960	Data centre	Germany	Central Archive for Empirical Social Research
UCLA Data Services	1961	Data library/service	USA	
ICPSR	1962	Data centre	USA	
Data Archiving and Networked Services (DANS)	1964	Data centre	Netherlands	Steinmetz Archive
Social Science Data Archives, Department of Sociology and Anthropology, Carleton University	1965	Data library/service	Canada	
Princeton Data Service	1965	Data library/service	USA	
Data & Program Library Service, University of Wisconsin-Madison	1966	Data library/service	USA	Data & Information Services Center (DISC)
The Institute for Policy and Social Research	1966	Data centre	USA	
UK Data Archive	1967	Data centre	UK	UK Data Service
Data Library/Service RAND Corporation	1968	Data library/service	USA	
Electronic Records Division, US National Archives	1968	Data centre	USA	NARA Data Archives Program
Odum Archive, University of North Carolina	1969	Data centre	USA	The Odum Institute

For many of these services, storing, managing and sharing code to analyse and interpret the data was as important as preserving the datasets themselves. For example, the name of the centre at the University of

Wisconsin was the Data and Program Library Service (DPLS). This was established as early as 1966 by the social science faculty. Its major functions were acquiring, storing, maintaining and preserving machine-readable data files and the computer programs that were used to analyse data files. In addition to its library functions, it also acted as a social science data archive that preserved and disseminated studies created by the university social science faculty. DPLS was a special library on campus, run by a faculty director, completely separate from the University of Wisconsin Library System. DPLS changed its name to the more modern DISC in 2007, following a merger with other specialized data services.

A succession of data librarians at Wisconsin have been graduates of the School of Library and Information Studies (SLIS) at the same university, bringing cross-disciplinary synergies between the library field and the core social science disciplines – politics, economics, sociology and demography – that make up DISC's active user base. Indeed, SLIS under the direction of Jane Robbins in the 1980s and 1990s was considered to be part of the social sciences, with a focus on humans' use of information, and a doctoral programme that emphasized data collection and analysis. Unsurprisingly, one Director of SLIS (and Assistant Director of DPLS) between 1969 and 1986, Alice Robbin, was a lecturer in both the Economics Department and SLIS. After getting a PhD in Political Science there, she went on to have a varied career in social science research and eventually settled at the School of Library and Information Science, Indiana University, where she no doubt instils methodological rigour in students taking her research courses.

A number of North American data libraries are now co-located with map libraries, or employ data librarians who are also geographic information science (GIS) specialists (or may not be called data librarians at all). Duke University Libraries provides an interesting example, with its Data and Visualization Services. According to its website, the service 'provides consulting services and instruction that support data-driven research. Our team of consultants and interns offers support in data sources, data management, data visualization, geographic information systems, financial data, and statistical software. Our lab includes 12 workstations with the latest data software . . . and is open nearly 24/7 for the Duke community' (http://library.duke.edu/data/about).

Other US data library services emerged from government documents library services, which in providing access to government information found they needed to be expert at statistical reference as well, and then to provide access to social science datasets. A case in point is Northwestern University Library, which offers 'Government and Geographic Information and Data Services' (www.library.northwestern.edu/libraries-collections/evanston-campus/government-information).

North America and the accidental data librarian

As we can see, just as data libraries have emerged from a variety of organizational environments, so too the profession of data librarian or archivist has been built up by largely pioneering individuals coming from a variety of professional backgrounds. While many come from the library profession, which in turn is known to be over-represented by those with humanities undergraduate degrees, others come from the social sciences, GIS, statistics and IT backgrounds. Moreover, each individual or group of professionals has put their own stamp on the profession, contributing their knowledge and talents, be it in metadata and knowledge organization, government sources of numeric data, data analysis and statistical software, survey methodology, or spatial data and GIS. Although many data librarians love their work, very few have felt they are on a steady career path. This sentiment led to a popular session at the 2005 IASSIST conference chaired by Cindy Severt, 'Discovering a Profession: the accidental data librarian', which was followed up by a lively blog post on the IASSIST website (Humphrey, 2015).

The accidental nature of the profession has made the task of educating a cadre of data librarians difficult, and devising a professional certification scheme nearly impossible. As a professional membership organization IASSIST has struggled with the concept of education for data librarianship over the years and has largely taken a pragmatic approach of professional development via workshops at its annual conferences, loosely co-ordinated by an Education Committee. In their 2010–14 strategic plan, IASSIST members showed concern about the lack of formal education for the profession, but decided this was best taken forward by university library and information science programmes or iSchools, with the association lending support: 'Formal education for data librarians and data professionals is ad hoc and not widely available in member countries. As an association of data professionals, many of whom have been trained within the association, the organization should strive to work with higher education institutions to formalize data training' (Herndon et al., 2010, 12). Certainly members of IASSIST appear in the programme of the 2013 conference held by the European project DigCurV, 'Framing the Digital Curation Curriculum' (Cirinnà, Fernie and Lunghi, 2013).

Other notable contributions to training for data support or data librarianship by IASSIST members include the DLI Train the Trainers workshops in Canada; the DLI training repository records materials from 1996 to the present (cudo.carleton.ca/collection/dli) and week-long training for data librarians at the ICPSR summer school, which dates back to 1974. More recently ICPSR and UKDA staff have collaborated to offer the training on both sides of the pond. RDM training for librarians is more recent, and will be looked at in Chapter 3 and elsewhere.

Europe and the convergence of user support and reader services

One of the essential characteristics of traditional librarianship is devising procedures and documentation that allows discovery and use of printed collections within established disciplines or categories. This is commonly known as reader services. For those working with digital data collections there was initially a different emphasis. This was on the development of user support and helpdesks to deal with questions or enquiries from researchers wishing to use specific archived material. Most data archives saw them as an essential step in the days when advice was needed on how to work with complicated and obscure data formats or technical tools. Over time the data have become easier to use and manipulate because of the developments already outlined and in particular the widespread adoption of common statistical analytical tools such as SPSS, Stata and R. At the same time the work of archival helpdesks has expanded and started to follow a path familiar to most librarians. User support in archives has come to cover a wide range of activities such as answering general enquiries, advising on what data collections to use, promoting newly available data deposits and resolving specific problems in using data a researcher may encounter.

European data archives played a central role in supporting academics using data for their research while also encouraging preservation. However even this has changed, as recent developments in academia encourage a wider interest in data preservation and verification. Data repositories are of course well placed to deal with this but academic libraries themselves have also begun to take an interest. So as data archives have sought to emulate the reader services role of academic libraries, the latter have also begun to emulate the role of user support.

This can be seen in the increase in the number of data librarians now being appointed at major academic libraries and the inclusion of data curation and preservation into the work of reader services. (For a crude estimate, Figure 1.2 shows the number of jobs posted to the IASSIST jobs repository from 2005 to 2015. This demonstrates increases over the decade except during the recession of 2008 through 2010.) Another important factor in the movement of data services into libraries has also to do with periodic economic recession and its impact on academia generally. As funding became unstable one option to ensure survival – and even growth – has been to merge with academic libraries. The more stable funding of the latter plus shared interests in resource purchasing and support encouraged this development. Overall, then, the increase in the number of data librarians in the USA and Europe can be seen as an important response to changes in research practice, funding and research innovation.

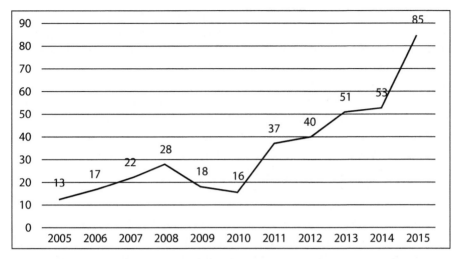

Figure 1.2 *Jobs posted to the IASSIST jobs repository, 2005–2015*
Source: IASSIST (www.iassistdata.org/resources/jobs/all).
Posts can only be submitted by members, so jobs reflect the membership and their organizations, mainly in the USA, Canada and Europe.

National archives give way to academic libraries

This chapter has outlined many of the different factors that have combined to encourage the development of data librarians in academic libraries. The final influence to note is the shift in how governments, funding bodies and other stakeholders view the long-term future of data archiving. This change has happened in the last ten years and particularly affected the European model, most notably in the UK. The focus appears to be shifting away from centralized national data archives as the main location for preservation and dissemination of raw research data. Existing archives continue to expand and receive funding but there is now a stronger commitment to encourage institutional data repositories. These are intended to hold and share research data produced within a specific university rather than on the basis of subject or discipline. This follows the lead of developments in publishing such as the open access movement, where copies of publications are now being collected and archived at an institutional level. Many publishers now require that the underlying data of publications be preserved, discoverable and accessible at a repository, with reciprocal links between the article and the data. This is discussed further in Chapter 2 as part of the discussion of citation of data.

A new map of support and services for researchers

The sum effect of these developments is to create a need within universities for trained information specialists who are able to pull all these strands together and advise on collections development and the use of data that are being preserved. There is also a need for those experienced in liaising with researchers when accessing the archived data or creating the data from scratch as part of their research practice. Libraries and their data librarians are ideally placed to address these needs.

This is only the starting point for a basic understanding of what constitutes data librarianship. It is an evolving blend of traditional librarianship skills, such as advising on resource discovery on the one hand and providing background on specific issues of data formats or digital obsolescence on the other. On some occasions it may require the application of detailed specialist knowledge about collections or undertaking analysis. At other times it may require providing advice on copyright, managing data as part of the research process, or selecting the most appropriate data analysis tools. It is certainly not the case that a data librarian has to be thoroughly grounded in every aspect of digital scholarship or data manipulation. We have fortunately moved on from the situation in which specialist assistance was needed from computing experts simply to unpack data from storage and then access it in a usable format. It is now possible for researchers to access great volumes of data directly through a web browser or catalogue record. Sometimes specialist IT advice may still be required but in many cases analytical tools are even provided at the point of access.

The understanding of how the overall system works or where to find these sources of data is what may be missing for researchers. So on many occasions a librarian who can demonstrate a familiarity with some of the key issues and knowledge of which specialist to recommend within their own institution will be playing an important part in supporting research practice.

As Mary Auckland has noted,

> Libraries will need to respond to this challenge by developing a unique role – in consultation with their institution – for the part they will play in the support of meeting researchers' information and related needs. The research environment is changing, driven not least by the power of technology to transform the way they work. Libraries are largely in uncharted territory, and have the chance to draw a new map of support and services for researchers.
>
> (Auckland, 2012, 78)

Key take-away points
- Research data that are collected as part of a research project, described and made available for use by other academics are referred to as datasets.
- Techniques for supporting research data have been formed around practical problems of storage, discovery and access, and are dependent on the technical solutions available.

- Data librarianship – like IT-based data support – has been shaped by cultural norms to do with research funding, institutional expectations and academic practice.
- Early research data support was defined by requirements for specialized technical expertise but this need has perhaps receded as technology has changed and improved.
- The demand for research support is not limited to information discovery and access but calls for deeper engagement with the research process.
- Archives and data libraries developed to support specific datasets – such as government surveys – incidentally facilitated the accumulation of academic research project data.
- Initial services were focused around physical media and methods of delivery. As online technology spread the dominant theme has become access.
- Many academic libraries kept research data support at arm's length but many now grasp its strategic importance and have established data services.
- Focused technical expertise is useful for a data librarian to have but so is a familiarity with the range of scholarly communication issues and appreciation of the wider academic context.

Reflective questions

1. Which of the two historical models most closely mirror your own institution or region – the North American or the European?
2. Will you support research data exclusively, is it one resource type among many you will deal with or is it something you would expect to pass to another service or unit?
3. What expertise does your background give you that would be useful in providing data support?
4. What do you favour in responding to innovations in research: a strong grounding in analytical techniques or skills in information discovery and consultancy?
5. What are the benefits of social research that uses either a quantitative or qualitative approach?
6. What do you consider to be the top three datasets available to your discipline?
7. Would your own institution include datasets in its main catalogue? What criteria does it use? Should this change?
8. Why have many data libraries been set up outside the academic library? What are some of the benefits of locating the service in the library?

CHAPTER 2
What is different about data?

Attitudes and pre-conceptions

The daily work of the data librarian can be quite similar to that of our more traditional named academic librarians. It can involve working within library systems, acquiring resources and developing working relationships that allow you to promote the role of your library. The fact we work with research data alongside periodicals, books and other publications should not make that much of a difference to how our work is seen but for a variety of reasons it does. The word 'data' itself is off-putting to some traditional academic librarians and researchers and a cause of some anxiety. For some it is because it seems to belong to other disciplines and have little relationship with their own work. Others see it as being such a common word as to be almost indistinguishable from 'information'.

A good example of these different perspectives can be seen in the social sciences. Researchers that use survey techniques and questionnaires create a body of data that can be recorded, analysed, summarized in the form of statistics and, in due course, form the basis of publications. They are clear that this is their dataset and appreciate its role in enabling analysis. It is numerical, quantitative and quite obviously 'data'. On the other hand researchers using qualitative techniques such as semi-structured interviews or focus groups create a body of work that includes audio transcriptions as well as perhaps audio recordings or photographs. This material is just as crucial in informing analysis but within that tradition it is routinely not perceived or referred to as 'data'. A similar situation can be seen in many disciplines within the humanities (Ward et al., 2011), which focus on working with 'primary materials'. Within visual art research a similar resistance has been noted so that there is, 'An additional task to those working towards the same ends in other disciplines: the translation of scientific RDM concepts into language meaningful to those working in creative arts disciplines' (Guy, Donnelly and Molloy, 2013, 101).

Data librarians need to be aware of these nuances if they are to be successful in promoting RDM. Reflection on the attitudes you encounter and adopting the terminology of different user communities will be important in offering effective support from your library during a research project. It will also influence the related work you should do in promoting data as a significant research output in its own right after a project has completed.

The digital dimension

It is interesting to consider some of the ways different types of data are distinguished or held to be different from those in other disciplines. Increasingly most research uses digital technology and the fact data are being created or analysed in the digital realm provides a solid foundation. If something is digital it is machine-readable and therefore potentially open to analysis by software; it may also be 'human-readable'. Even so this simple shared platform (the computer) is often overlooked and instead types of data are grouped in opposition to each other. Quantitative data are contrasted with qualitative data. Big data are contrasted with small data (or long tail data as we shall discuss later in this chapter). Text and numeric data are separated and in turn held apart from real time data such as audio recordings or video clips. All of these can represent forms of research data at one time or another, depending on the research objectives.

Some resources developed by research support agencies – or as part of an academic institution's efforts to create a research support infrastructure – focus on these issues by attempting definitions of research data. Some select definitions include:

- 'The recorded information (regardless of the form or the media in which they exist) necessary to support or validate a research project's observations, findings or outputs' (University of Oxford – http://researchdata.ox.ac.uk/university-of-oxford-policy-on-the-management-of-research-data-and-records).
- 'That which is collected, observed, or created in a digital form, for purposes of analysing to produce original research results' (University of Edinburgh – www.ed.ac.uk/information-services/research-support/data-library/data-repository/definitions).
- 'Research data: The data, records, files or other evidence, irrespective of their content or form (e.g. in print, digital, physical or other forms), that comprise research observations, findings or outcomes, including primary materials and analysed data' (Monash University – http://policy.monash.edu.au/policy-bank/academic/research/research-data-management-policy.html).

- 'The recorded factual material commonly accepted in the scientific community as necessary to validate research findings' (University of Southern California – http://ooc.usc.edu/data-management).

The Research Data Strategy Working Group in Canada produced a report, *Mapping the Data Landscape*, which noted: 'The concept of research data is complex and fluid. Virtually all types of digital information have the potential to be research data if they are being used as a primary resource for research' (Research Data Strategy Working Group, 2011, 4). Clearly a comprehensive working definition is always going to be elusive since it has to encompass research in many disciplines based on a wide variety of traditions, presumptions and working practices. Institutions and repositories with a relatively narrow focus of research – perhaps within one discipline – can coin definitions in more detail. In cases such as the University of Oxford any definition needs to be basic because of the wide range of disciplines involved.

Reaching an operational definition
The definitions of research data cited above are good starting points but the changing contexts in which material is used plays a more important role. For example we would argue that there is a situational aspect to defining research data and whether one conceives of research material as data depends on what you wish to do with them. Examples noted in the online data management course Research Data Management Training, known as MANTRA (http://datalib.edina.ac.uk/mantra), include 'a photographic image of an old municipal building in a historical archive is an archived image in an image bank. But when used by a researcher to study the history of a city, the photographic image becomes data for that researcher.' So regarding something as data may be just as dependent on the purpose or timing of the use of such materials as its content.

The case is similar for data collected and compiled as part of the process of governance or management by governmental bodies or large commercial enterprises. These data were not collected with future research in mind, but are now beginning to be seen as a potentially useful source of untapped knowledge and insight. The data were, after all, collected systematically and in a rigorous structured manner. This type of material has come to be called administrative data, or 'process-produced data'. In the UK access to administrative data from government and the voluntary sector was initially arranged by the Administrative Data Liaison Service, which defined this material as, 'Information collected primarily for administrative (not research) purposes. Government departments and other organizations collect this type of data for the purposes of registration, transaction and record keeping, usually during the delivery of a service. In the UK, government departments are the main (although not exclusive) purveyors of large administrative databases, including welfare, tax, health and educational record systems' (www.adls.ac.uk/adls-resources/guidance/introduction). The Administrative Data Research Network has now replaced this service.

There are many other examples of how what constitutes data is 'in the eye of the beholder' and therefore the way researchers or other stakeholders define research data varies. In most situations it is best advised to work with a description that works best in practice. This operational definition should be consistent with local institutional policy on data and align with the purpose of your data management services. For example, if your service will only concern itself with supporting digital data, you may not want to adopt a definition that includes physical objects, even though they may legitimately be considered data in another context. The data librarian should also try to think about how these definitions will help as a framework for typical questions they will encounter regularly.

Is there a difference if data are created or re-used?

The origins of a data collection or dataset is often discussed as if it has some key role in defining its validity and future use. But does it? In the social sciences the method of 'secondary analysis' (re-analysing existing data with different statistical techniques or from a different theoretical model) provides a rich vein of scholarship. However, in the social and natural sciences there also persists an attitude that original research involves collecting or creating original data for analysis. Many undergraduate politics or sociology students want to base their research on data from their own surveys or interview projects – on data they have created rather than re-using existing data. The act of being newly created is what is perceived as giving the data value and relevance.

On the other hand, researchers in some science areas and in most humanities areas see their research as always involving the re-assessment, collection or compilation of existing materials and data. A research project investigating form and metaphor in the works of a leading poet or novelist will have a rich body of work to examine. As a result the researcher may argue they have produced no actual data in the course of their work. However, even something as seemingly straightforward as selected quotations, tabulations of keywords, digests or in fact anything that has restructured the source material in a new way prior to analysis could be seen as data. This failing to recognize that what they have produced as data is an illustration of how some disciplines may be viewed as completely untouched by the requirements of data management.

Any discussion of the value of data in terms of whether it has been created or collected is not really important. These are simply different kinds of material which data librarians will need to advise on at some point in relation to data management and long-term preservation, either early on in a research project when a proposal is being put together, or when a project is nearing completion or has even long since been archived. However, such discussions become important when they are used in an attempt to ignore or question the relevance of such advice.

Data and intellectual property rights

Intellectual property rights (IPR) are defined as rights acquired over any work created, or invented, because of the intellectual effort of an individual. The most routine form of IPR dealt with in libraries is of course copyright, but other forms include patents, trademarks, geographical indications, industrial design rights, design layouts and confidential information or trade secrets. Academics generally have a clear idea of how IPR affect their publications or other written research outputs, which is especially important as it can define their position as far as commercial exploitation and academic attribution is concerned.

A common question is whether data may be controlled by IPR in the same way. Once a research project has been concluded, the resulting research data should be treated as an output or series of outputs in much the same way as publications. As a result, it should also be covered by law on IPR and the message to communicate is that this is one of the mechanisms for defining how data may be managed, disseminated and re-used. This may include, where appropriate, by other academics, funding bodies, publishers and the public.

Researchers may wish to clarify this by asking who has primary ownership of the data. This can sometimes be a stumbling block as legislation on ownership of data can be unclear. We would argue that in most cases it can be more useful to rephrase the question into one about rights of use rather than ownership; whose rights should be considered when making decisions about the management and dissemination of data? Researchers are not familiar with having to think about data in this way, especially if they are not accustomed to making it publicly available. Institutional policy also needs to be considered, as universities differ in how they assert institutional rights to outputs and data from research conducted with their resources. Similarly, it should not be assumed that institutions assert ownership over data produced by staff and students in equivalent ways.

The type of data being collected or created also has a bearing on IPR. Photographs, videos or other recordings, for example, can be treated as original works, and clearly benefit from normal copyright protections. Spreadsheets on the other hand do not appear to fall within the same category. Lack of knowledge of IPR in the context of data has a tendency to make researchers conservative in how they view rights to their data as well as their accessibility.

Answers to these issues are often very context dependent because, 'The source of all IPR is national law. Certain international treaties harmonize intellectual property owners rights but leave the users rights to vary by country. Second, certain countries... [including those in the EU] have created a specialized database right that applies to certain databases created or maintained within their borders' (Carroll, 2015).

Databases may be protected by the 'database right' arising from the European Database Directive (1996), in recognition of the work involved in their creation, structuring and arrangement. One stipulation of the directive is that they do not need to meet the criterion of originality used for copyright protection. The database right also exists in countries outside Europe, such as Australia, but is not recognized in the USA.

Certainty about who has rights in data can create a great deal of anxiety in researchers. This feeling can be increased by a lack of clear guidance or policy on the part of an institution. When commercial exploitation is a possibility advice and guidance becomes clearer, but of course this does not apply in many cases. Confidence in this issue is also important as it has a direct bearing on who has the authority and responsibility for managing the data during and after the research project.

The relationship of metadata to data

Within libraries there is an established tradition of using metadata as the foundation of resource discovery and retrieval tools. This is descriptive information that is created to be machine-readable and sits alongside documentation that is designed to be human-readable. Increasingly the two terms are becoming interchangeable. Metadata can play an important part in the management of research data as well. So advising on this should be adopted as a particular responsibility of data librarians and data professionals.

Metadata generally refers to the adoption of a digital disciplinary standard that is useful for searching through large amounts of data such as Dublin Core schema (Briney, 2015, 50). For example metadata at the variable and value level describe in detail how each element has been collected, derived and coded. In some disciplines this view of metadata as a highly structured technical description is softened to include more general forms that document how data was created, originally used and the relationship of files. Metadata and documentation become synonymous. Examples are questionnaires, codebooks, experimental protocols, laboratory notebooks or information about equipment settings. As noted in guidelines prepared by the ICPSR regarding social science data preparation and archiving, 'Because it is often impossible for secondary researchers to ask questions of the original data producers, metadata becomes the de facto form of communication between them' (www.icpsr.umich.edu/icpsrweb/content/datamanagement/lifecycle/metadata.html).

So, when advising on preparing data for use outside the confines of the original research project and perhaps at some time in the future, it is important to stress that anything that provides context can improve comprehension and discovery by potential users. This is one of the ways in which datasets differ from other research outputs such as publications. The various conventions of writing a journal article or book chapter ensure that there is context given to the ideas and analysis being discussed. This is a basic part of communicating research findings. The principle of preserving and sharing data as a post-project objective needs similar grounding as does the production of related documentation and more particularly metadata. It is the responsibility of data librarians to communicate and promote these points (see Figure 2.1).

Figure 2.1 *Understanding that data (like fire) can be shared*

© XKCD Comics, 'Prometheus' (https://xkcd.com/1228/). Used in accordance with https://xkcd.com/license.html.

Many researchers make the mistake of assuming data they are making available for secondary usage will be used by others for projects with similar objectives and methodologies as their own. This is not always the case as the data may be used by researchers in related disciplines, or radically different fields, so any associated metadata that helps secondary users understand how the data were created and coded is going to be important. The data librarian may frequently be called on to advise on what is suitable metadata. In practice this may amount to suggesting the researchers assess what documentation they would normally produce and whether they think it would be a good use of time to produce anything additional. If a project is collaborative and involves a group then it is likely the appropriate documentation will already have been produced since a shared understanding of what data are being created will have been required.

Good and effective data documentation is always useful to the original creators of a research data collection. This is an important point for data librarians to make even if improvements can be made to it by data professionals in libraries, repositories and archives to make it optimal. Researchers may complain they are being expected to do more work to help others but they will always be the first beneficiaries as the original creators.

Organizations such as ICPSR, UKDA and the Digital Curation Centre (DCC) provide extensive guidelines on what constitutes effective and appropriate metadata, which can broadly be broken down into:

- descriptive metadata – enabling indexing, discovery and retrieval
- technical metadata – describing how a dataset was produced, structured or should be used
- administrative metadata – enabling appropriate access and management of the material.

Metadata standards are therefore another key area where the data professional or data librarian should take a lead. Most metadata standards are based on eXtensible Markup Language (XML) or the Resource Description Framework (RDF), which is in essence, plain text, therefore highly portable. As has been noted, 'Some people speak of XML and RDF as if they are themselves metadata formats, but this is confusion between *form* and *content*. Both XML and RDF are actually general data formats that can be used for any number of applications' (Coyle, 2005, 160). These languages can be used for marking up data so that it can be manipulated by software. Promoting a minimum set of expectations in the organization and content of metadata is an important part of developing a RDM infrastructure for an institution that builds on its researchers' concerns. This is because 'Metadata standards often start as schemas developed by a particular user community to enable *the best possible description of a resource type for their needs. The development of such schemas tends to be controlled through community consensus combined with formal processes for submission, approval and publishing of new elements*' (Higgins, 2007, our italics).

Most data archives produce guidelines on metadata standards and leading schemas such as Dublin Core and the Data Documentation Initiative (DDI). The DCC compiles information on disciplinary metadata standards, including profiles, tools to implement the standards, and use cases of data repositories currently implementing them (www.dcc.ac.uk/resources/metadata-standards). In addition there are projects such as ISA-Tools (www.isa-tools.org) that have been developed by Oxford's e-Research Centre. This is an open source set of metadata tracking tools intended to manage data from life science, environmental and biomedical experiments. However some disciplines do not

WHAT IS DIFFERENT ABOUT DATA? 27

have a consistent or clear set of guidelines on metadata. This may especially be the case in areas that do not encourage sharing of research data. Whatever the situation a data librarian should encourage researchers to become aware of what is most appropriate for their work.

Big data

Data librarians need to consider how to relate researchers and their data to established support and management frameworks such as copyright and IPR. They also need to think about emerging areas of interest and one of these is often described as big data. In a 2001 research note Laney, coined the 'three Vs' of big data, when he wrote of how many researchers were becoming encumbered by an ever expanding quantity of information. This was characterized by a number of new features that were just as important as the sum of material being amassed, 'Sea changes in the speed at which data was flowing mainly due to economic commerce, along with the increasing breadth of data sources, structures and formats . . . were as, or more, challenging to data management teams than was the increasing quantity of data' (Laney, 2012).

This led him to identify three orders of magnitude, which would help underline some of the key issues in managing such information and making the best use of its potential. First there is volume, which describes the simple fact that larger and larger amounts of data (relative to whatever is seen as a norm in any particular discipline) are being dealt with or produced. This is often what gives the content its value or potential in research. Second, velocity describes the speed at which it is being generated, processed or analysed. The third defining characteristic is variety, which means the data are not only diverse but also have incompatible formats or misaligned structures and semantics. Structured data may be collated with unstructured data and are seemingly difficult to use together. The challenge regarding variety then becomes one of managing this incompatibility in the most effective way. During a project work is ongoing to 'Organise newly generated data while cleaning and integrating legacy data when it exists, and deciding what data will be preserved for the long term. Although these actions should be part of a well oiled data management workflow, there are practical challenges in doing so if the collection is very large and heterogeneous' (Arora, Esteva and Trelogan, 2014, 17).

Since the 'three Vs' of big data were coined more have been added by others such as veracity, visualization, value and so on. These can sometimes be useful in describing the research data that are being produced but such terms may equally be applied to any data. They are also aspirational rather than dealing with orders of magnitude and it is the latter and how this is dealt with which is novel. Indeed, Greiner pinpoints this when she describes big data as 'Data that contains enough observations to demand unusual handling because of its sheer size, though what is unusual changes over time and varies from one discipline to another' (https://datascience.berkeley.edu/what-is-big-data/#AnnetteGreiner). The value of the three Vs, and the reason big data has been such a resonant concept, is that it highlights the practical challenges and potential specific to new channels of research data. A range of analytical developments that offer new opportunities for academia and business (Chopra and Madan, 2015).

Long tail data

The opposite of big data represents in many ways what most of us consider to be the norm in academic research. Data and activity based around small-scale projects lasting only for a few years and producing small volumes of material. Often these are based on the work of an individual or small research team. Logic would suggest this be termed 'small data' but in fact since it is often illustrated with graphs showing a steep drop in volume in the data that is produced – or tailing off – it has come to be called 'long tail' data (see Figure 2.2). Further description, in this case for neuroscience, is provided by Ferguson et al. (2014, 1442):

> Long-tail data in neuroscience can be defined as small, granular data sets, collected by individual laboratories in the course of day-to-day research. These data consist of small publishable units (for example, targeted endpoints), as well as alternative endpoints, parametric data, results from pilot studies and metadata about published data. The long-tail of data is also composed of 'dark data', unpublished data that includes results from failed experiments and records that are viewed as ancillary to published studies (for example, veterinary care logs). Although these data may not be considered useful in the traditional sense, data-sharing efforts may illuminate important information and findings hidden in this long tail.

The potential for making greater use of such material thanks to increased efforts to organize, preserve and share it lies at the heart of RDM. As is so often the case the data librarian does not necessarily need to become an expert

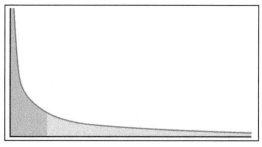

Figure 2.2
The long tail of research data

Picture by Hay Kranen, public domain (https://en.wikipedia.org/wiki/Long_tail). The graph shows a typical long tail distribution. The x axis is the size of the dataset and the y axis is the number of datasets. In this example, the cutoff is chosen so that areas of both regions are equal.

in the many forms of big data and long tail data that are taking shape. It is however important that the terms are at least familiar to those working in research support.

Why is this of interest for data librarians? These concepts have driven the development of data management as a subject. Big data in particular has attracted strong interest in academia, where the challenges of developing software or methodology to deal with it form part of many high profile projects. More on the challenges of big data can be found in Chapter 9.

The need for data citation

Although we are at pains to encourage the consideration of data as a resource and research output in its own right, the relationship with publications is of course important. Many researchers have made – and continue to make – data available via their own or institutional websites, often as a way of augmenting published findings. The problem is that URLs lack any real longevity and it is easy to lose access to data when there are broken links. One crucial development in recent years has been the ability to use permanent digital identifiers that allow citation of data, which emulates the citation of traditional published materials. These identifying codes allow citation of data that is effective because it is both discoverable and persistent. The Data Citation Principles of Force 11 recognize 'the dual necessity of creating citation practices that are both human understandable and machine-actionable' (Martone, 2014). The eight principles require that:

- there is equal *importance* of citing data with publications in backing claims
- wherever a claim based on data is made in scholarly literature, that data should be cited as *evidence*
- citations should give *credit and attribution* to all contributors of the data
- *unique identification* of data that back up a claim is possible
- a route to *access* be provided
- there is *persistence* to metadata and identification even after the data are no longer available
- there is *specificity and verifiability* such that an empirical claim based on the data can be interrogated and repeated
- a balance of *interoperability and flexibility* must be achieved to allow use both within and across homogeneous communities with different citation practices.

DataCite is an international collaborative organization that promotes data citation through dissemination of digital object identifiers (DOIs) for datasets, a form of persistent identifier common in published literature (just as CrossRef disseminates DOIs for journal articles). In practice DataCite works with data repositories and libraries, which manage their own DOIs (these are purchased through an annual membership fee). According to their website, 'data citation is fundamental as it enables easy re-use and verification of data, making it possible to track and quantify the impact of data' (www.datacite.org). Even if the location of a data collection changes, the identifier will remain the same – as long as the owner of the DOI updates the registry. Guidelines produced by the UKDA note that data citation:

- Acknowledges the author's sources
- Makes identifying data easier
- Promotes the reproduction of research results
- Makes it easier to find data
- Allows the impact of data to be tracked
- Provides a structure which recognises and can reward data creators.

(http://ukdataservice.ac.uk/use-data/citing-data)

The benefit of this to researchers is tangible because it means academic profiles can be built up and measured by citation not only of publications but also of data.

Publishers have been aware of these developments and see it as another way of boosting interest in journal articles and other publications. Data citation is also discussed in terms of providing links to 'the underlying data' of an article or 'the data behind the graph'. This trend is in fact expanding with journals such as *Nature* offering to host archives of 'underlying data'. Increasingly publishers are making it a condition of publication that the location of data related to an article is made clear by an author. The Nature Publishing Group policy states, 'Supporting data must be made available to editors and peer-reviewers at the time of submission for the purposes of evaluating the manuscript. The preferred way to share large datasets is via public repositories' (www.nature.com/authors/policies/availability.html#data). The Public Library of Science (PLoS) group of journals also has a similar policy and states, 'Providing more specific instructions for authors regarding appropriate data deposition options, and providing more information in the published article as to how to access data, is important for readers and users of the research we publish' (http://blogs.plos.org/everyone/2014/02/24/plos-new-data-policy-public-access-data-2). Accordingly the data librarian may also receive requests for assistance in clarifying these issues. These will not be discussed in terms of wider data management or data sharing but rather as publication and publisher issues. Nevertheless they have wider importance as such requirements represent proxy demands of readers who would otherwise be unable to access the data. These are often requirements of researchers that would not have been considered during the original research project. Data citation may also be seen as another step away from informal exchange of data 'between colleagues', which often characterizes academic discussion within departments or at conferences towards a more formal framework of data sharing. For many academics these issues can be an introduction to the idea of ensuring that research data are preserved, discovered and accessed once a project has been completed and when it is no longer under the stewardship of the original research team. The issue of data citation is crucial and will be returned to in subsequent chapters.

Embracing and advocating data curation

Research funding councils, data archives and institutional repositories are actively encouraging the curation of research data. But what does this mean? Curation encompasses the active policies and procedures needed to preserve research materials outside the framework of an original research project and beyond its original (short-term) objectives. It was for this reason, for example, that a London School of Economics (LSE) project laying the foundations of institutional data curation was called 'Sending your data into the future' (http://learningresources.lse.ac.uk/168). The passage of time presents many of the greatest threats to digital data. This ranges from loss of understanding regarding data content to digital obsolescence, which renders data files unreadable. A study of data-sharing practices commmon with US astronomers between 1999 and 2014 showed that more datasets were being linked to articles but also that the availability of linked material decays with time (Pepe et al., 2014). Ongoing procedures and actions on data and metadata – in other words curation – is therefore needed to maintain, preserve and indeed add value to data collections throughout the whole of the data lifecycle (see Figure 2.3).

Figure 2.3 *A simple data lifecycle diagram emphasizing curation*
© DCC, used with permission.

Data curation is similar to the curation and preservation of print and other collections that libraries and museums are engaged with daily. The role of the data librarian has to include encouraging or curating digital data as well. This is a necessary response to the increased interest in identifying, preserving and sharing research data by funders, institutions, publishers and most importantly researchers. The data librarian has to develop a degree of judgement in how to handle these sometimes complementary and competing interests. In some cases it is the research team that curates the data over time. More often this work is carried out by staff of a data archive or a repository, in which case advice on finding a sustainable host may be needed. The more homogeneous the data collection the more it can benefit from applied curation (for example adding controlled vocabularies or ontologies). As in the case of providing definitions of research data there is no 'one size fits all' approach.

The work of a data librarian can be equally situational; in some circumstances the data librarian may simply aim to support researchers' approaches to data management, leaving the choice of methodology or data formats to a research team for example. On other occasions, it may be better to be more assertive and give firm guidelines on what data formats to use if those being discussed are clearly lacking, potentially obsolescent or limited in re-use potential. Similarly there are situations in which a data librarian needs to consider data collections as preserved resources requiring long-term investment, from the point of view of funder requirements or institutional policy, and manage the collection. Ultimately it is this requirement for the exercise of judgement in advising on data management and data curation for research data creators, users and other stakeholders that makes the work of the data librarian so stimulating.

Key take-away points

- Data are most commonly numeric but they may include information in any form created as the result of a research project.
- Data may be newly created or collected from and derived from existing sources.
- Data require management and curation to ensure effective use and longevity.
- Considering how best to manage data means that someone has to take responsibility for them.
- Documentation and metadata have taken on new importance and can be taken as a particular focus of interest for data librarians.
- Leading data support organizations such as the ICPSR, UKDA and the DCC provide guidelines on what constitutes effective and appropriate metadata.
- Familiarity with developments as a driver of expectations regarding research support is often all that is needed – not expertise in every data-related development.
- Standards have been developed that allow citation of data collections and as an additional output of a research project.
- One of the greatest threats to using or understanding data is the passage of time.

Reflective questions
1. What are typical presumptions about 'research data' in your discipline and do they need adjustment?
2. Is it better to have a flexible definition of data so it can be responsive to the questions you may encounter in your institution?
3. Are there particular areas of managing research data that cause anxiety for researchers in your field? If so how can you provide effective support for them?
4. What strategies can you use to make researchers aware of the benefits of data management to their own research and not simply as something that assists others?
5. Do you have policies and mechanisms in place that encourage data citation?
6. Will you encourage data management infrastructure that assumes most of the work will be done by the original researchers or your institution – or a combination of the two?
7. What do you see as your role: helping researchers manage data for their project or developing something that will become an institutional resource?

CHAPTER 3
Supporting data literacy

Information literacy with data awareness

Academic librarians have excelled in promoting the information literacy agenda and developing bibliographic instruction as part of learning research skills. Not only is it quite common for library sessions to be a key part of new student inductions, but examples abound of successful partnerships with university instructors for getting library-based training into the classroom and coursework, and sometimes even assessed. Virtual learning environments, online courses and distance learning all offer new ways for librarians to interact with learners and teachers as well. A little bit of 'data awareness' can go a long way in extending traditional information literacy and bibliographic instruction programmes.

In some ways existing forms of library instruction lend themselves easily to the addition of concepts of data management and re-use. For example, in teaching about doing a literature search in a given discipline, librarians may give instruction in using standalone or online reference management tools, such as EndNote, Reference Manager, Zotero or Mendeley. For some disciplines in which the data used are mostly in textual form (e.g. law, history), such tools may even be the best method of conducting data management throughout a research project. For disciplines using other data types, further organizing options may need to be explored, such as those described in the Research Data MANTRA training course Organising Data (http://datalib.edina.ac.uk/mantra/organisingdata).

Bibliographic search methods may also be useful for teaching skills in data discovery. Students will not find all of the references needed for a literature search solely by consulting Google or Wikipedia, nor will they find all the supporting non-textual data for their research that way. Data librarians can teach the use of specialized data portals, disciplinary data centres, government statistical websites and repository registries alongside the use of specialized publication databases to aid discovery of published literature and data. Besides, in the case of many online databases, licensed products, or datasets requiring permission to access, content cannot be indexed by Google, and so familiarity with potential sources is essential. Training in data sources may be offered to particular classes or as part of information skills programmes. Alternatively web-based resources may be offered, for example the Bodleian Data Library web pages (www.bodleian.ox.ac.uk/data).

Students can also be taught to look for citation trails to key datasets through publication lists of seminal articles. For example, where a publication has been written that is based on an original dataset, the author should provide instructions for obtaining the dataset for re-use, if not a complete citation to it. If nothing else the author's contact details may be used to track down an incomplete reference to a dataset (or the data librarian can help by contacting the author on behalf of the student). Some data repositories (such as ICPSR and the UKDA) offer lists of published articles and papers associated with datasets in their collection. These are especially useful for determining whether a line of enquiry has yet been pursued on a given dataset, for example to help determine an original research topic.

Promoting data citation

One area in which data librarians and others can easily incorporate data-aware information literacy in their instruction is by instilling the importance of data citation. At its essence, data citation is simple, and analogous with textual publication citation: in order to stand one's own work up to scrutiny a proper reference list must be provided, with enough detail for the reader to track down the relevant content of the referenced object. Just as one would not dream of putting a reference such as 'Smith, 2013' in a citation list or bibliography, it is surely unacceptable to print a table with the caption 'OECD, 2013' with no further citation appearing in the reference list. Yet this has been common and accepted practice until quite recently.

What has changed? As shared datasets, images, video clips and other non-textual digital objects become more valued in exchanges of scholarly communication in their own right, the provenance of these objects gradually becomes as important to the scholarly record as the peer-reviewed, published papers which describe and analyse them. This is not only important for the reader who wishes to track down a copy of the original object; it is equally important for the object's creator who wishes to receive career rewards based on the academic value of their work, as measured through citation counts and other impact measures that show the data have been recognized, consulted, downloaded or cited in other studies (including replication studies).

So data librarians wishing to support best practice in information literacy can advocate 'proper' data citation along with well established bibliographic citation practices, stressing not only that it should be done but also advising on how it can be done. Some but not all major style guides provide assistance in how to cite data, so in many cases applied judgement is required. An interest group of the IASSIST has created a short, practical Quick Guide to Data Citation (www.iassistdata.org/community/data-citation-ig/data-citation-resources), which provides examples based on applying the general principles of three major style guides to an agreed set of minimum citation elements.

Data citation can be trickier than bibliographic citation as the data can vary so much: for example, citing small fractions of large datasets, citing a constantly changing database or map, citing underlying data elements going into a compiled dataset or data visualization, or perhaps citing an unpublished data object that has been shared informally. Some of these problems are being tackled by the research community, such as various working groups of the Research Data Alliance. Others can be solved through good examples. Statistics Canada has made a useful attempt to provide citation guidance for a number of different forms of data: tables, maps, graphs, published and unpublished datasets, e.g. microdata and custom tabulations (Statistics Canada, 2009). Good practice is encouraged by the fact use of their data for published analysis is conditional on proper citation. The guidance is also useful for building a citation for data of various types from any provider (Statistics Canada, 2009).

Most of what has been said above applies to human-readable citations. However it is just as important to be able to have machine-readable or computer-actionable citations. A website address or URL is an example of the latter, because it provides the means to access the reference (through a hyperlink or by pasting the string into a web browser). However the problem with URLs, as we have all experienced, is that they change or disappear – they do not tend to persist. The Hiberlink project carried out by Los Alamos National Laboratory Research Library and University of Edinburgh in 2013–15 investigated the extent of 'reference rot' – defined as a combination of 'link rot' or '404 Not Found' errors for URLs – and content drift, in which the referenced web page has changed its content or underlying structure since the citation was given. The project found that overall, 'One in five articles suffer[s] from reference rot' (Burnhill, Mewissen and Wincewicz, 2015, 56). One existing solution used by many publishers is to instead use persistent identifiers (or IDs), such as handles or DOIs, which provide a mapping from the URL to a persistent ID maintained by a central facility. This improves the chance that a resource will be found as well as fixed in an unchanged state, but only if the content continues to be hosted somewhere and the mappings are updated as websites change or publishers merge or go out of business.

The Data Citation Index, by Thomson Reuters, is an example of a newer service which tracks data citations, though its impact on the academic community is not as well established as its sister service for publication references, Web of Science. A few alternatives also exist. Google Scholar has the merit of being free and more widely accessible. Also, it does not discriminate between textual publications and datasets, as long as it recognizes the source of the dataset as a publisher (such as a repository). Altmetrics and related services may also help to make the impact of data creation and citation more visible.

Finally, remind students to cite the data they create or collect themselves! This is 'Rule 5' from 'Ten Simple Rules for the Care and Feeding of Scientific Data': 'Link Your Data to Your Publications as Often as Possible. Whether your "data" include tables, spreadsheets, images, graphs, databases, and/or code, you should make as much of it as possible available with any paper that presents it. Your data can even be cited before (or without) its inclusion in a paper' (Goodman et al., 2014, 3).

Data discovery

Established researchers often know what datasets are available in their field of study, or at least the main sources and providers from which to seek them. They are immersed in the literature and knowledgeable about the activities of their peers, they know the institutes and principal investigators that are producing research relevant to their work. This is usually not the case with postgraduate students, even less so with undergraduate students, and nor is it the case with researchers exploring the boundaries of their disciplines or doing cross-disciplinary research. Fortunately for data librarians, it is possible to become knowledgeable about sourcing datasets in a given field without being an expert in that field. A simple prompt or series of suggestions of possible avenues to explore enables them to be in a position to come to the rescue of researchers needing to source existing data.

Clearly data librarians will provide online guidance for data discovery as well as offer face to face support. Existing data libraries offer wonderful examples of creative online outreach material of all sorts. Just to give two examples from the authors' own workplaces, there is a library guide 'Data and Statistics for the Social Sciences' from the University of Oxford (http://ox.libguides.com), and the portal Finding Data from Edinburgh University Data Library (www.ed.ac.uk/is/finding-data). As both of these lean towards social science data, here is another example by Brian Westra, University of Oregon Libraries: 'Chemistry – Handbooks, tables and reference data' (http://researchguides.uoregon.edu/c.php?g=366305&p=2475534).

Staff and students may be reluctant to schedule a face to face appointment asking for support for various reasons, so making them aware you are available for consultations in a variety of ways is useful. Scheduling office-hours, drop-in sessions or surgeries is one approach. Building relationships with teachers and supervisors of research students is another: helping teachers to construct a data-related assignment, introducing a special resource in the classroom, or putting a reference list in a syllabus are all ways to make your service known and contact details readily available to inquiring students. By offering support to teachers you may also be encouraging them to raise their game in teaching by providing live data sources, in turn encouraging students to create their own research questions and to learn how to answer them.

One of the authors was involved with a large UK study on barriers to the use of data in the classroom in social, geographic and health-related disciplines, those thought to be the biggest users of secondary data, from February 2000 to June 2001. In institutions with no dedicated data support service, the situation is unlikely to have changed very much:

> The survey uncovered a number of barriers experienced by teachers in the use of these services, namely a lack of awareness of relevant materials, lack of sufficient time for preparation, complex registration procedures, and problems with the delivery and format of the datasets available. These problems were elaborated in open-ended comments by respondents and in the case studies of current teaching practice. . . A compounding problem is the lack of local support for teachers who would like to incorporate data analysis into substantive courses. A majority of the survey respondents said that the level of support for data use in their own institutions was ad-hoc. Peer support was more common than support from librarians and computing service staff, and over one-third received no support whatever. The top three forms of local support needed were data discovery/locating sources, helping students use data, and expert consultation for statistics and methods (for staff).
>
> (Rice and Fairgrieve, 2003, 19)

The good news for librarians is that here is a demand that can be readily addressed in the form of support for data discovery. Albeit, the demand may have to be stirred up where academics do not expect data support to come from the library. In Chapter 5 we explore further how libraries can begin to establish credible research data services where they have had none before.

Data reference interviews

Once the enquiries are coming in, whether from undergraduates, postgraduates or academic staff, how do data librarians match users to the data required, to make liberal use of one of Ranganathan's Rules: 'Every reader his book' (https://en.wikipedia.org/wiki/Five_laws_of_library_science). The answer is largely already known to the trained librarian – through a reference consultation or interview.

The trick to giving reference interviews well is to realize that the question or data query being asked by a user may not be exactly what is required. Through a process of active listening and prompting for more information using open and closed questions, the librarian is able to translate the user's initial query into a question that can be looked up using available sources. By avoiding shortcuts, jumping to conclusions or making assumptions, the librarian spends a little extra time getting the query right, and saves the time of the user by finding the answer to the right question instead of an irrelevant one. An example is a UK-based researcher who asks how to log on to get data files from ICPSR, when what she really wants is access to the Canadian Election Surveys microdata files, which are available freely on the web as well as from the ICPSR and a number of other data providers. Even this example is simpler than most, because the researcher already knew the title of the dataset she required. Data-related queries tend to be more difficult, more time consuming, and sometimes even bewildering to the non-subject expert trying to provide assistance to the experienced researcher. The following advice was given to organizational representatives of the UKDA in 2000 (primarily librarians and IT support staff), with respect to conducting data reference interviews:

> There are a few angles that data supporters can take in leading a reference interview. First, be sure to determine the level of enquiry the user is committed to undertake (tactfully, of course). Is the work for a complex analysis or a class paper? Will it be part of a planned research project lasting several months, or background statistics for a quick and dirty proposal with an encroaching deadline? Is the user experienced with using secondary data or a novice? Is s/he well-grounded in the subject or methodology, or traversing new terrain? What statistical packages is s/he prepared to use? You are likely to encounter some users again (and again) as they progress through the stages of their analysis; others may have just a one-off request. Finding out this information at the outset will help you anticipate future needs, and will prevent wasted efforts, such as referring users to published sources when they want the raw data, or ordering data files when all they want is a printed table from a book.
>
> (Rice, 2000, 8)

In order to help a user find an appropriate dataset to answer a research question successfully, you may need to prompt the researcher for further information about their requirements, such as:

- general subject or research question
- unit of analysis (e.g. country or other geographical area, household, individual, company)
- key variables required
- required format of the values (e.g. is age by year essential or do age groupings suffice?)
- dates or years required, whether very recent data are required or not.

In practice, if the researcher is starting with an original research question rather than a known study or dataset, it is likely they will be forced to make trade-offs about all of the details they require: for example, settling for an older date of collection than wished, or a larger geographic area than desired, or a proxy variable because data for the preferred variable do not exist. Factors that affect the need to settle for such trade-offs include amount of time the user has allocated to complete the work, their level of data analysis proficiency, willingness to struggle with a raw dataset, and perhaps whether they have the qualifications to apply for use of more sensitive datasets with special conditions.

For example, to apply for Eurostat microdata, which requires completion of an application form and a confidentiality agreement before access, the user must also present proof they are a member of staff of a recognized research entity. After submitting the application they must wait a number of weeks for each country's statistical agency to sign off their approval of the research project before they are given a copy of the data. In many cases the researcher is unaware of these hurdles at the beginning of the process, and you may find yourself needing to manage expectations or locate a less ideal but more accessible source.

Categories of data

It is enormously helpful to narrow down the type of data required at an early stage, especially if microdata – data about individuals – or macrodata – data aggregated at a higher level, such as country or region, are expected. A user seeking 'labour statistics' or 'data on fertility', for example, may require either. Further discussion is needed.

If the research question requires survey data (responses from questionnaires), could a single, one-off survey or poll answer the question or does it involve change over time? If the latter, the options may be limited to known survey series that repeatedly sample the population at different points in time – (known as cross-sectional surveys, such as *British Social Attitudes*).

However, a study of social mobility, for example, may require data points at different times in individuals' lives – such as their parents' occupation at birth, their grades in school, whether they completed higher education, and their salary or occupation at a given age. Perhaps only longitudinal studies, where the sample is made up of a constant set of individuals who are traced over time, can address these sorts of research questions. Examples include both panel studies such as the UK's long-running household panel study, *Understanding Society*, and 'cohort' studies, which follow a sample of a particular generation over time, often from birth, such as *Growing up in Scotland*.

Another category of data, often consulted by economists and business researchers, is known as time series: as the term implies, these data usually consist of a single variable over several points in time, often arranged in columns, whereas comparisons (e.g. between companies, equities, countries, regions, etc.) are listed in rows. Data queries requiring time series often begin, 'I need data for X (variable) going back 20 years/quarters/months, etc.'

Geospatial data, on the other hand, focus on comparing one or more variables for different but comparable regions, government districts, zones or countries, often using a standardized code, such as the European NUTS 1, 2, 3 (where the numbers represent varying geographic sizes of regions), Census codes, or postal code. This will also often come in a row and column format, with geographic names or codes in the rows, and variables – often including an X and Y geographic co-ordinate – in columns. Often the researcher will wish to use the geographic co-ordinates to map the data, for example in a GIS analysis package, often by adding a new layer to a base or topographical map that shows some basic features. The researcher may build their map either with points (for example, to represent the centre of the region) or boundaries, in which case the extent of a numeric value can be displayed in shades of colour (this is called a choropleth map). There may or may not be a time series component, but if there is, this would normally result in more than one map.

Top tips for the reference interview

Since every research question is unique (unlike every classroom assignment), it is easy to feel daunted when confronted by a new one. These are some helpful hints to guide you through a difficult reference interview:

- Buy yourself time by asking more questions before trying to come up with a source; avoid making assumptions about the user's requirements, prior knowledge or viewpoint.
- Find out if the user is basing their query on a published article; ask for the citation or a copy to help you with the context. If a student, ask who is their teacher or supervisor.

- Ask the user to explain acronyms and jargon they use in their language; you do not have to pretend to be an expert in their area of study to help them.
- Take notes and write down key phrases as the user speaks (if meeting in person or on the telephone).
- Even if you are unable to find the perfect source for your user, you can probably give them some useful starting points for their search, based on your knowledge of data sources, or that of your peers.
- Do not be afraid to take time to think, search and consult others; always take the user's e-mail address for future contact or to follow up.
- If you remain stumped, resort to asking others: immediate colleagues, peers at other institutions, government statistical agencies, data providers and publishers. Once you have done your homework and ruled out obvious contenders you can also post to a library mailing list or the member list of IASSIST.
- If the query is about using a dataset rather than finding one, take time to read the documentation, try out the interface yourself or reproduce the problem before turning to others for help.
- If the user does not voluntarily let you know their query has been satisfied, follow up in a reasonable amount of time to see if you can offer further assistance.

When doing data reference work there are often ample opportunities when helping a user discover or work with data one on one gently to improve their understanding and skills in data literacy. While you are looking up data resources, for example, speak aloud about why you are going first to this source (government agencies often have authoritative data on this subject) or that source (the UKDA has very good metadata for searching at the variable level), so the student learns how to evaluate data from different sources.

Many datasets and published databases are useful to researchers and students because of the statistical content they contain. In the case of microdata (individual-level data with cases displayed as rows and variables displayed as columns), summary or descriptive statistics must be created from the microdata through statistical analysis or spreadsheet software. In the case of data taking the form of pre-compiled descriptive statistics – aggregate data – such as some government statistical serials, the descriptive statistics have been produced for public consumption. This may be in the form of tables and charts. Regardless, the user needs a basic level of statistical literacy in order to make best use of the information received. A higher level of statistical competency might be required if the published tables are not up to the task of answering the research question and so the original dataset needs to be queried directly, for example to produce new tables from a single year of age instead of age groups, or with a cross-tabulation of two variables that do not appear in the pre-compiled version.

What has statistical literacy got to do with it?

How is statistical literacy related to data literacy? There can be no single answer to this question in these fast-changing times, but the IASSIST social science data library and archives community has long held the notion that to be data literate one must be both numerate and possess some level of statistical literacy. Numeracy has various definitions but is sometimes treated in common with functional literacy – the ability to do basic arithmetic, or perhaps the absence of numbers anxiety. In addition to being able to manage one's household budget and other common tasks associated with adult numeracy, news media commonly convey numeric information about rates, ratios and percentages – so a non-expert level of numeracy is essential for responsible citizenship. For students and researchers to learn to be comfortable using numeric data sources they must in the first instance be numerate or 'comfortable with numbers'.

Statistical literacy goes beyond basic numeracy to being able to understand and evaluate statistical results as they appear in research literature. It is not necessarily as deep a knowledge as statistical competency or proficiency. In part it means simply being able to understand information displayed in tables and graphs. It also involves understanding other statistical concepts well enough to judge the claims being made in research literature. Examples include understanding how response rates, sample types and sizes contribute to the accuracy of statistical claims, and measures of statistical 'significance', or the likelihood that finding a given result is not due to chance, as commonly expressed in P values. Furthermore, to critically understand statistical claims that others make (which could be one definition of statistical literacy), it is necessary to understand how a sample was selected or chosen, and therefore whether or not it is representative of a larger population. (Note that this is the kind of additional documentation that the original data creator or claim maker needs to provide to make the data understandable and the analysis comprehensible.)

Unfortunately many statistical concepts – to do with odds, chance, randomness and probability – must be learned, and are simply not intuitive. As David Spiegelhalter, a statistician at the University of Cambridge who specializes in conveying concepts of probability to the public, has wryly written, 'Why do so many people find probability theory so unintuitive and difficult? After years of careful study, I have finally found it's because probability is unintuitive and difficult' (Spiegelhalter, 2011).

Milo Schield, who established and edits the website Statistical Literacy (www.statlit.org) aimed at improving the statistical education of undergraduates, claims that what information literacy, statistical literacy and data literacy have in common is the evaluation of information: 'All librarians are interested in information literacy; archivists and data librarians are interested in data literacy. Both should consider teaching statistical literacy as a service to students who need to critically evaluate information in arguments' (Schield, 2004, 6).

In studying the behaviour of his own business students at a liberal arts college in Minnesota, Schield has made a number of interesting observations about the tendencies of statistically illiterate readers. For example, when reading a research article, some skip over tables and charts, preferring to take in the information in narrative form. Unfortunately, much of the critical thinking involved in judging the importance of tables and graphs comes from studying all of the elements going into the visual display of the numbers.

Bear in mind it should be easier to teach statistical literacy, skills to evaluate statistics used as evidence in scientific and social arguments, than full statistical competency. To be statistically competent one must know how to apply statistical techniques correctly to research problems, which requires more knowledge and experience. Combined with a healthy dose of critical thinking, teaching statistical literacy can even be fun. What nonsense can occur from reading row percentages when only column percentages make sense? What fun can be made of looking at completely unrelated variables that have 'statistically significant' correlations simply by coincidence? Statistical fallacies are commonly found in news media articles oversimplifying scientific results, such as equating correlations with cause and effect. Similarly, 'bad' charts can be critiqued for common tricks such as not starting the Y axis at zero, or otherwise exaggerating small differences.

There is no shortage of material for this kind of training activity. Full Fact (fullfact.org) is one dedicated organization, based in the UK, which focuses on statistical and other kinds of fact-checking to correct misleading claims by journalists and politicians about current affairs. The home page has a range of recent news stories corrected or confirmed. Academic blogs by critical thinkers, such as David Colquhoun's Improbable Science (www.dcscience.net), can be useful sources as well. Ben Goldacre, a physician and blogger on Bad Science (www.badscience.net), has been so successful at this sort of critical writing he first became a *Guardian* newspaper columnist and then a best-selling author.

Data journalism and data visualization

Data journalism sites such as the Guardian's datablog (www.theguardian.com/data) offer good examples for making statistics visually compelling, and telling stories with data. Data visualization sites like Flowing Data by Nathan Yau (flowingdata.com) and Information is Beautiful by David McCandless (www.informationisbeautiful.net) are equally inspiring. Indeed, students' attention may be captured more easily with workshops on data visualization or data journalism than data or statistical literacy per se. Duke University Libraries Data and Visualization Service (http://library.duke.edu/data), as the name indicates, foregrounds data visualization tools and workshops along with topics in data analysis and data management. Studying and creating infographics may be another way to capture the imagination of students who are reluctant to learn about statistics.

Topics in research data management

Until research funders began promoting the importance of RDM – and sharing, as a way to increase efficiency of scarce funds for a growing scientific agenda in the last decade (see Chapter 7) – the support that did take place occurred in a very individualistic way, and was hardly taught by anyone, let alone librarians. So it is not surprising that data librarians may need to work to create demand for such training. However basic data management principles and practices are not difficult to teach, and can easily be incorporated in an information literacy training programme. The overlap with furthering open access to publications and the desirability of getting datasets into the preserved scholarly record should be enough to justify the inclusion of RDM in the information literacy training programme, especially for postgraduates, who are likely to be creating new datasets in some form. As with open access, librarians are in a position to affect academic culture change, which unlike rapid technological developments can be notoriously slow. Presenting the benefits of good practice in data management and sharing to early career researchers and students before less desirable habits are formed is one way to speed it up.

Fortunately, there are many benefits of undertaking data management, especially for researchers who have never considered it in a conscious way before – not least, avoiding the disaster scenario of losing all of one's research data owing to lack of a back-up plan. If this seems unlikely just go do a Twitter search on 'lost USB stick', and you will no doubt find similar messages to the one shown in Figure 3.1, which appeared in an Edinburgh neighbourhood newspaper, the Broughton *Spurtle*, on 16 August 2015.

Of course the number of topics to address in RDM training partly depends on the length of the training, the audience and indeed the trainers; librarians are comfortable with slightly different subjects from those taught by IT professionals or statisticians, for example. The University of Edinburgh conducted a training programme in RDM for its academic service librarians in 2012–13 covering topics that it was agreed were within the sphere of the librarians' professional interests and, potentially, areas in which they could provide support for researchers or training for students. These were:

- data management planning
- organizing and documenting data
- data storage and security
- ethics and copyright
- data sharing.

Data management planning is perhaps the most important topic on which to focus. (There is more about support for data management planning in Chapter 6.) The other topics focus more on the practice of managing data throughout the project and what is involved with sharing data – presumably at the end of their project, after a thesis has been written, or a paper has been published. Of course, data management plans are not always required for postgraduate research; it is much more common to be required by a funded grant. So unless you are able to work with the graduate schools of departments to require a data management plan (DMP) of some kind as part of a thesis proposal, training on writing a plan aimed at students may be little more than awareness raising. However, by covering the other practical topics – many of which students are unlikely to be exposed to in their postgraduate training – they will be more likely to pick up the immediate value of what they are being taught.

Figure 3.1 Lost USB stick
Source: www.broughtonspurtle.org.uk/news/please-help-find-lost-usb-stick.

The closer the training can come to their actual experience of working with data, the better. If students want to learn how to organize a database efficiently, they will not be interested in the finer points of using a lab notebook. If they are compiling information from textual references for a paper about changes in policy or legislation over time, they will not wish to learn about how to transform image data from one format to another. This is why subject librarians can be invaluable partners in designing and delivering appropriately focused data management training.

While designing domain or discipline-specific data management training can be time consuming as well as challenging, many lessons in data management really can be presented in a more generic fashion. This is because there are commonalities across domains for working with data as evidence or as proxy for ephemeral content (a dance performance) or analogue content (rock samples from a geology field trip). Part of what is common is the digital nature of the data. As disciplines have gradually 'gone digital' in their practice, academic lecturers naturally continue to emphasize the subject content of doing research rather than the practicalities of working with similar data in digital form, or with new tools or software. It is therefore sensible for data librarians or IT professionals to focus on the digital nature of the data and the skills needed to work with digital material – both data and code.

What does a well rounded data management training programme look like? The University of Edinburgh's open, online RDM training course, or MANTRA, is well used by those wanting to brush up their data management skills in a range of disciplines, and is employed by institutional trainers in many countries to supplement face to face and other bespoke training.

MANTRA consists of eight main topics, each designed to take about an hour to step through, and including interactive quizzes, video clips of researchers describing how they have dealt with data management issues, and further reading. An additional section on data handling extends the skills into working within four particular software environments. On the 'About' page of the MANTRA website (http://datalib.edina.ac.uk/mantra/about.html) the primary benefits for research students of taking the course are listed:

1. Understand the nature of research data in a variety of disciplinary settings
2. Create a DMP and apply it from the start to the finish of your research project
3. Name, organise, and version your data files effectively
4. Gain familiarity with different kinds of data formats and know how and when to transform your data
5. Document your data well for yourself and others, learn about metadata standards and cite data properly
6. Know how to store and transport your data safely and securely (back-up and encryption)
7. Understand legal and ethical requirements for managing data about human subjects; manage intellectual property rights
8. Recognise the importance of good RDM practice in your own context
9. Understand the benefits of sharing, preserving and licensing data for re-use
10. Improve your data handling skills in one of four software environments: R, SPSS, NVivo, or ArcGIS.

Although there is a nominal ordering of topics, MANTRA is designed for mixing and matching, letting readers dip in and out of topics of interest – one strategy for coping with learners from a wide variety of backgrounds.

The avatars on the home page guide users at varying career points towards suggestions of topics to look at first. The inexperienced research student who may not have worked with data before is pointed towards 'Research data explained', which introduces the wide variety of research data in existence, with a smattering of disciplinary approaches to using data. The career or postdoctoral researcher is already well immersed in data use, but may not have written a DMP before, so is pointed to 'Data management plans'. The senior academic, who is experienced in all stages of a funded research project and supervises postgraduate students, is pointed towards 'Sharing, preservation and licensing', because they may be less familiar with publishing data than papers, and towards the 'Data handling tutorials' in case they can use them in a practical workshop with their students. A fourth avatar is for the information professional, who may have the most to learn in the unit on data protection, rights and access, but may also be interested in organizing a few colleagues to study in a small, supportive group by using the 'DIY Training Kit for Librarians'.

MANTRA was one of the early arrivals of RDM training, launched in 2011 as the deliverable of a funded project in the first Managing Research Data Programme of Jisc, a UK provider of higher education services, and regularly updated by the Data Library team at EDINA, Information Services, University of Edinburgh. Training materials in RDM are now abundant, and some excellent training materials can be found on the RDM pages of several institutions. We list here a few highly recommended training resources or portals; readers are asked to observe copyright and licensing conditions when re-using materials:

- DCC's Resources for Digital Curators at www.dcc.ac.uk/resources.
- New England Collaborative Data Management Curriculum at http://library.umassmed.edu/necdmc/index.
- DataONE (Data Observation Network for Earth) at www.dataone.org/education-modules.
- FOSTER (Facilitate Open Science Training for European Research) training portal at www.fosteropenscience.eu.
- IASSIST Resources: Data Management and Curation at http://iassistdata.org/resources/category/data-management-and-curation.
- companion page for the UK Data Service's book *Managing and Sharing Research Data*, with related presentations and group exercises at www.ukdataservice.ac.uk/manage-data/handbook (Corti et al., 2014).
- Essentials 4 Data Support, from Research Data Netherlands (in English or Dutch) at http://datasupport.researchdata.nl/en/.
- RDM and Sharing MOOC (massive open online course) at www.coursera.org/learn/research-data-management-and-sharing (a free Coursera MOOC developed and delivered by the University of North Carolina-Chapel Hill and the University of Edinburgh for researchers and librarians. A certificate of completion is available for a small fee).

Training in data handling

Research students may agree to study topics in data management but what they really want to be doing, and therefore learning, is how to analyse their data. The reason the ninth module of MANTRA focuses on data handling skills in particular software environments is that the authors saw data handling as an intermediate skill between generic data management skills (which overlap with basic computer literacy) and data analysis – which is more domain-specific and normally taught within a curriculum.

Data handling, or data manipulation, is at the heart of pre-analysis data preparation – such as data cleaning, recoding and creating documentation, merging files based on common variables or cases, or exporting from one type of software and importing into another without losing data content (format migration). It is equally at the heart of post-analysis processing – preparing a 'golden copy' master of the data on which results are based for long-term preservation, documenting changes made to data files, and depositing in a data repository in an appropriate format.

Data librarians who provide help with research datasets in particular software packages tend to have or acquire excellent data handling skills. They are in a good position to provide training in these skills, the very skills which tend to get left out of curriculum-based data analysis courses and IT-based 'introduction to X software package' workshops.

Depending on one's background, there are a number of attractive data-related training courses that data librarians can and do offer their local communities. By partnering with others in the library or IT centre, academics or even outside the university, such as local or central government, one can combine knowledge to provide extremely attractive data-related skills-based courses.

Just a few imagined examples include Preparing a Successful Data Management Plan, Working with [the latest] Census Data, Data Visualization Basics, Mapping Your Data, Data Journalism 101, Data Preparation and Analysis in [insert your favourite software package here], Preparing your Data for Publication, Sharing Your Data for Impact, Making Your Research Reproducible and Keeping Your Data Safe.

Reskill yourself

There are many opportunities to not only create training but also receive it yourself. School of Data (http://schoolofdata.org) is an open educational resource that focuses on the skills needed to use government-linked open data, and 'works to empower civil society organizations, journalists and citizens with the skills they need to use data effectively – evidence is power!' Data Carpentry 'develops and provides data skills training to researchers' based on the successful model of Software Carpentry. Data analysis and visualization in R, OpenRefine for cleaning datasets, database management with SQL (Structured Query Language), and coding in Python are hot topics currently covered by Software and Data Carpentry. Various summer schools focus on honing data-related skills as well. ICPSR and the UKDA often host summer schools in data analysis and data support in Ann Arbor, Michigan, USA, and Essex, England. The Research Data Alliance (RDA) and CODATA (Committee on Data for Science & Technology) have begun hosting a week-long School of Research Data Science in Europe, as well. Sources such as Lynda.com offer multiple online training tools in various kinds of software. Conferences such as IASSIST, iPRES (International Conference on Digital Preservation) and the International Digital Curation Conference offer pre-conference workshops on data and curation-related topics.

Supporting data literacy is an ongoing objective of the data librarian. It will also involve the use of skills that raise your profile with researchers and deepen your involvement with their work in many cases. Inevitably the skills that stead you well now will go out of date or need augmenting. Keeping up your own data literacy involves not only going to conferences, reading the literature and monitoring trends on social media, but actually learning new skills. Data skills are bound up with software skills. Software is not static, but changes with each new edition of the program, introducing new capabilities, and dropping others deemed no longer to be necessary, and you must keep up with these changes. Also, software at its essence is code; there's no avoiding learning a bit of coding to handle data well. If you insist that you are 'not a programmer' you will not only limit yourself forever to the limitations of graphical user interfaces, but you will also miss some wonderful opportunities to interact with young people who are coming together to share skills in open source communities. Although some of these initiatives may not be coming from the perspective of a researcher, they all share enthusiasm for the data-driven world we are inhabiting, and a desire to be in control rather than controlled by it. As a data librarian, learning on the job is a necessity – but also a privilege.

Key take-away points
- Basic data literacy can be incorporated in mainstream library instruction and information literacy training.
- Librarians and data librarians are in a position to promote good data citation practice, even where examples in style guides are lacking.
- A relatively easy way for data librarians to help researchers is in sourcing existing datasets.
- Incorporating live data into a teaching setting is time consuming; data

- librarians may be able to assist those in teaching roles by creating fit-for-purpose teaching datasets.
- ➤ As with reference enquiries, data enquiries need not be taken at face value; dig for additional context before trying to answer the question. Follow up to find out whether the information offered was useful or more help is required.
- ➤ By being aware of different data types (published statistics, microdata, macrodata, survey data, longitudinal data, geospatial data), the data librarian is better equipped to match a researcher with an appropriate data source.
- ➤ Numeracy is the bedrock on which statistical literacy can be learned. Statistical competence goes beyond being able to critically understand statistical claims, to being able to make them.
- ➤ Data management planning helps keep a research project on track from start to finish – avoiding disasters such as lost data.
- ➤ Data librarians can cover a range of data management topics, appropriate to the level and discipline of the group – from planning, to file management, to documenting and controlling versions of data, to storing and transporting data securely, to legal and ethical requirements of data collection, to applying metadata for sharing and preserving data. Free, vetted training resources on these topics abound.
- ➤ Challenge yourself to learn new data-related tools and software. Take time to play with data.

Reflective questions

1. Why is it becoming more important for researchers to cite the data they use in their work?
2. How might you approach a teacher to offer your support to their students in the use of datasets?
3. What do you consider is an appropriate amount of time to devote to a data enquiry?
4. Which do you think is more important for being statistically literate: numeracy or critical thinking skills?
5. Which data management topics would you be comfortable teaching yourself, and which would you call in an expert or colleague? To which groups at your institution?
6. How can you fit learning new data-related skills into your schedule?

CHAPTER 4
Building a data collection

Policy and data

A task faced by many data librarians is the acquisition and development of digital resources in the context of a larger library of printed material. This can be done through adoption of a range of procedures but there are also benefits in having a formal written policy. A formal description acknowledges that a policy fulfils many functions beyond being merely a tool for choosing materials. In addition to describing current collections, it encourages 'the staff involved to (re)consider the aims and objectives of the organization, both long and short term, and the priorities to be attached to different activities. It assists with budgeting, serves as communication channel within a library and between the library and outside constituents, supports co-operative collection development, prevents censorship, and assists in overall collection management activities' (IFLA, 2001).

Development of a formal policy is recommended and it ought to encapsulate the range of activities to be undertaken by the data librarian. It will involve selection of materials of course but will equally build on the relationships with readers within a department and library, mechanisms for promoting resources and receiving feedback, and raising the profile of your work within the larger organization. The policy needs to acknowledge that collection development can be different where data are concerned.

Data as a resource to be acquired

What are the various issues to consider? Many traditional topics to do with library print collections apply equally to those of us who are building up digital research data collections. Some institutions may regard the latter as more the responsibility of IT services or archival holdings if a digitization project has been involved, but the continuing evolution of academic libraries makes it important to stake a claim for responsibility in this area. In *Data Basics*, a seminal monograph on developing data libraries and support services, Geraci, Humphrey and Jacobs argue, 'The role of the library is to Select, Acquire, Organize, and Preserve information, and to provide Access to and Services for that information. Although some librarians question these roles in the digital world . . . these are the activities that define a library. If an organization fulfils all these roles . . . what would we call it but "a library"?' (Geraci, Humphrey and Jacobs, 2012, 65).

Data collections are increasingly considered resources to be managed as part of wider library collections and in much the same way as printed material. Some of the tasks associated with this may be specific only to print and physical media – such as binding repair, physical stock management or weeding of multiple and surplus copies. A key point to consider is that much digital acquisition does not involve physical objects or even ownership of digital files. What is often acquired is some form of access – or membership of an access group – as part of an agreement with a vendor. Free access to government data sources follows a similar pattern and has some of the same issues regarding control and convenience. Access may be easy to provide but this is not the same as holding or controlling data in such a way as prevents future withdrawal of service or changes to content. This creates a new set of management decisions. Even so some management tasks are similar for both print and digital collections – such as selection, promotion and monitoring of use.

Acquisition of datasets in itself is of course a key activity. This may include a range of data collections, which will need to be funded or subscribed to annually like many other library resources. So budgets need to be allocated and spent. Judgement must be developed in deciding what datasets need to be acquired and this should be based on understanding the immediate needs of a reader and appreciating trends within particular disciplines. In fact we would see this need also as the result of the fundamental distinctions between theoretical and empirical research orientations, especially in key departments such as economics, political science, sociology as well as medicine, business and others. Many data librarians may have their own requirements to address within collection policy – tailored to their own policies or those of their institution. Key resources that are seen as essential for a discipline or as cornerstone assets in any collection might also be considered. There may sometimes be difficulties if some of these are beyond your budget.

Subscription resources that are sold to academia and the commercial sector – such as company and business intelligence databases – tend to be the most expensive, even with concessionary pricing for academic use. So it is not uncommon to build up a wish list of resources and slowly work through it pursuing individual resources as funds become available. An alternative approach is to assess what is already being supplied by your institution and then look for missing elements or look out for resources which may be available in limited form. For instance there may be data purchased by a specific school, department or research centre under terms which restrict access to students and staff in that department. News of such resources spread quickly within an institution – especially as data are cited within publications – and expectations about access need to be dealt with diplomatically.

A recent example at the University of Oxford involved a patent database referenced in a presentation. This triggered a request to the library for access to the database and a query as to why it was not listed on any catalogues. Further investigation revealed the database was in use within a specific research centre, could not be made more widely available and that it was in fact paid for by a different institution collaborating on a project. After some discussion it was agreed the library could take out a subscription to allow wider access. Whenever it is an option it is wise to take these subscriptions into the library, so that all students, faculty and staff in the institution can access them. After all, it is almost always university funds paying for such resources, so access should not be restricted. Such limitations will represent missing provision for those without access. One part of collection development then becomes in effect thinking about current and future gaps in provision and how they should be remedied.

Promoting availability of resources

Not all datasets or resources are based around a paid subscription model although this will look the most familiar to librarians. Since so much good quality data are being made available through open access data portals they might also form part of a collection. This could involve simply promoting their availability and making readers aware that they can be used. The fact they are accessible at no cost is an additional benefit. In other cases it may be more effective to download the data and make them available locally within your institution. Especially if the data are enhanced – such as by providing syntax files, alternative formats, or even an online analysis service. This would involve having actual digital materials on your server with the consequent responsibility of curating and monitoring use. Whatever approach you take, these will be important steps in developing your core data collection, a range of data assets that will go a long way in defining your work, interests and most probably the support service you will be providing.

As is the case in traditional library collection development, it is often necessary to balance old and familiar items in a collection against the acquisition of new material. Mechanisms (such as web forms) that capture requests for new resources and then allow you to evaluate them will be necessary, and in a sense act as another aspect of promoting availability. Such mechanisms may be integrated with regular subject liaison work and simply involve promoting the fact requests are willingly received. Promotion of this sort may involve inviting e-mails, adding 'suggestions welcome' sections to websites or something as straightforward as a comments and recommendations book left in public areas. The objective is two-fold: to let readers know data – or access to data – can be acquired by the library in the same way as any other resource and that the data librarian is the person to contact. Requests may range from data collections that can be obtained at little or no cost, to resources which may have annual subscription costs running into the tens of thousands. Expectations should not be raised unrealistically and it is often important to note that while recommendations are sought, there is no guarantee the requested item will be obtained in every case.

There are a number of ways that requests for new datasets can be assessed once holdings have been built up. A collection development policy may already have identified weaknesses in a collection that need to be addressed and new requests could be considered from this perspective. Alternatively the number of requests a particular resource attracts might be captured over time. A single request in some cases may be enough to lead to an acquisition – especially if it is inexpensive or lies in an area you were already thinking of developing your collection. There may also be concerns that a dataset acquired for a single reader may not be used by anyone else in the future. Things are clearer if something is being asked for repeatedly and this will of course strengthen its case as a resource to consider.

If an acquisition with a cost attached is being considered it is usually advisable to arrange a trial, or period of limited access, to see if it attracts usage and to assess how well it is received by readers. Doing this can have the additional benefit of improving relations with departments and offering an example of initiative in support of their data needs. The experience of setting up the trial can in itself be instructive, as you are able to gauge the quality of service provided by the data supplier. This can be another factor in making a decision about acquiring a dataset. Trials do carry risks however. Time and effort is needed to promote the resource and a trial can often be inconclusive. It is not uncommon to arrange trial access to a product that seems to be in great demand and then receive very little feedback on how it performed or how it has been used.

Conducting trials is a mechanism which, once again, cannot on its own provide a conclusive argument for buying a data product. A data librarian needs to make the final decision based on the results of trial, what funding is available, whether it fits in with areas of research support that need to be improved, or simply whether refreshing collections would be useful. Often seeking opinions from other data professionals with more experience of the product can be useful. (The IASSIST membership e-mail list is well known and highly regarded for this community function, for example, but other specialized e-mail lists can also be useful.)

Data as a resource to be managed

Every acquisition should be viewed as an asset that will require future management and curation. It has been remarked that, 'In the case of digital data there is no such thing as the "benign neglect" of the printed era, in which old books could miraculously be rediscovered after many years in dust-ridden attics. Digital information is entirely dependent on a properly functioning hardware and software environment' (Angevaare 2009, 4). So an ability to maintain access over time will be important. Tasks centred on usage are also valuable in managing digital resources in much the same way as with print collections. For example, thought should be given to how frequently existing collections are being used. Unfortunately, how this can be done is sometimes problematic.

The frequency of lending of physical media can be tracked and movement of material off shelves can be counted. Requests for a copy, or even multiple copies, of books on course reading lists can be compiled. The virtual nature of digital datasets makes it difficult to compile usage statistics in the same way. Some data may be accessed via a publisher platform or interface created by a data supplier. Alternatively some may consist of a discrete database that is stored by a library and made available on request – such as a DVD or a local online resource. Whatever the access mechanism being used, it is not necessary to worry about how many copies to get or which will be normal and short loan copies. A database may be used countless times during the course of a term or semester without generating requests for additional copies to meet demand. Unlike a single copy of a printed resource it may even be accessed simultaneously by multiple users. Overall gathering intelligence on usage, especially of online remote digital resources, can be more challenging.

It is possible to access dataset usage statistics in some cases if vendors of a resource offer this as a service within a subscription. They may collect number of users or visitors to their website and provide useful information on activity. Such figures may be sporadic in nature, however, and it is worth checking on availability, mode of access and frequency. Blanket coverage of a range of resources is seldom an option – unless the data are supplied by the same vendor. Even in these cases the statistics can be limited in nature and may lack detail needed for planning. For example, reactions to evidence that a database has been accessed 200 times by users may be good, bad or one of indifference in the absence of information about the number of repeat users or length of engagement. So where usage statistics are provided by vendors, they may have a limited value, unless they are extensive. If used in combination with other criteria they may provide useful additional evidence in maintaining or dropping a data subscription. In practice such statistics are generally most useful as a last ditch and final confirmation that a dataset subscription could be dropped.

Luckily there are other options in assessing usage of datasets that make up for the deficiencies of some vendor-provided usage statistics. Data resources are virtual in nature and as a result are usually promoted virtually through websites, browser-based catalogue entries and included in web-based library guides. Tools such as Google Analytics allow a data librarian to collate statistics on what web pages are being accessed and what links selected, compared with the rest. This may in turn be combined with other useful usage indicators such as e-mail traffic and direct requests from users or departments. Responding to questions about accessing particular datasets that are already on the library catalogue, or obtaining access to datasets available elsewhere, is a common part of the work of the data librarian (see 'Data reference interviews' in Chapter 3). This may be seen as vital intelligence about potential demand for resources as well as the data needs of a single researcher. This underlines how often issues of data resources and resourcing can be linked to arranging data access.

Promoting and sustaining use of a collection

Every day, new books, journals and conference papers become available in print. Weekly lists of academic book publications are offered to legal deposit libraries in the UK. The Bodleian Library at the University of Oxford is a place of legal deposit and these weekly lists include 700 titles on average. At certain times of the year this number can go into four figures. Consideration therefore has to be given to how resources are promoted when acquired and over time when they become an established part of a collection and are in danger of being overshadowed by new additions. The size of weekly legal deposit lists demonstrates that the frequently referenced data deluge (Hey and Trefethen, 2003; Little, 2012; Wootson 2015) is also being accompanied by a flood of academic book and journals. As a result it can be an even tougher task to promote current or newly acquired datasets and data resources as they vie for attention with more traditional outputs. Nevertheless promotion is an important activity.

Existing promotional channels should be used rather than thinking of new ways of marketing datasets. If lists of newly acquired print titles are distributed then datasets can be added to them too. If departmental meetings are used to promote the work of the library, a section or standing agenda item may be added on new data updates. Where researchers have successfully lobbied for a particular dataset to be added to the range of collections available, this acquisition may be publicized and similar future interaction encouraged. Despite these efforts, however, a data librarian may quickly become used to hearing the comment, 'Our department didn't realize you bought this kind of thing!' Even so, it is just as important to put effort into managing and promoting datasets as it is to funding and acquiring them.

The quality of the documentation and cataloguing that describes datasets also demands attention as part of overall management and promotion of a collection. This can sometimes be difficult to do in systems developed to describe physical objects organized according to location. Nevertheless attempted harmonization is preferable to creating separate catalogues. Ideally documentation should be consistent and on a par with metadata being created for printed materials. It needs to use the same language so as to allow browsing and discovery. Digital collections need to be catalogued in a similar fashion as any other resource, in other words. This does not always happen. Some data resources – especially those with their roots as software programs – are regarded as analytical tools and therefore may not be included in library catalogues. Increasingly however it is common for such tools to be augmented with commentaries or analytical overviews and reports. As a result they have evolved into fully fledged information resources to be promoted in the same way as other academic assets.

Examples in the field of economics provide a good illustration of evolution from tool to resource and include products such as Datastream, Eikon and Bloomberg Professional, which provide client–server software for access to financial data. (Typically, in a client–server arrangement a server, or host, operates one or more programs, which share their service and content with users' own computers as separate clients, typically via a web browser.) In the geosciences there is software, such as the geospatial data tool ArcGIS and its non-proprietary alternatives, which functions as an analytical instrument but also produces advanced maps and visualizations. Data libraries will slice and dice categories of data in different ways in their online presence. For two cross-Atlantic presentations (there are many more), see the LSE Library's Data and Statistics page (www.lse.ac.uk/library/collections/featuredCollections/dataAndStatistics.aspx) and the University of Alberta Libraries data page (http://guides.library.ualberta.ca/data).

The importance of discovery

What other objectives can characterize the work of a data librarian? Improving the profile of digital collections and making them as discoverable as published textual materials is one of them. Discovery can be complicated by the different formats that may be involved. Some datasets may take the form of directly downloadable data and documentation files such as those supplied by the ICPSR in the USA or GESIS – Leibniz Institute for the Social Sciences in Germany. However others may be supplied as downloadable content available only in specific reading rooms or on particular devices according to the licensing restrictions imposed by the data suppliers. Examples here include information products based on derived information developed by companies such as Proquest or Bureau van Dijk, which package the information within their own user interfaces or dashboards to create resources such as the International Bibliography of the Social Sciences (IBSS), Orbis and Bankscope. Additionally, licensing agreements with some publishers or data suppliers restrict viewing of material to specific devices or locations, for example via an Internet Protocol (IP) address range.

As there are different ways of accessing subscription resources imposed by licensing conditions a hybrid approach to developing collections and establishing catalogues may need to be considered. Despite our earlier advice against establishing new catalogue and discovery mechanisms, a compromise may sometimes be necessary. At the University of Oxford, the Bodleian Data Library (www.bodleian.ox.ac.uk/data) was established as a new web-based discovery tool that outlines the nature of available data and the various ways they may be found and then accessed. It is also a useful collection management tool because during its development it established the boundaries of the collection, helped give it shape and highlighted possible gaps in provision. The website is intended to be used in conjunction with older and more local web-based finding aids at Oxford (called SOLO [Search Oxford Libraries Online] and Oxlip+) but also has a useful function in allowing advocacy and feedback for data-related issues among its target audience.

The mode in which users actually engage with data collections or deal with usage limitations varies greatly in practice. This may be frustrating for those who are used to the idea of digital resources being available on demand or on a variety of devices. Data librarians need to be aware of potential user frustration and prepare to manage collections in such a way as to reduce the impact of limitations. This was one of the ancillary objectives of the Bodleian Data Library when describing the wide range of collections available. When researchers find out about what data resources are offered it ought to be done in such a way as to minimize these differences and presenting all the resources – at least at the discovery level – as one of a range of unified and harmonized assets and part of a coherent and well developed collection.

Building on researcher liaison

What other elements can contribute to building a data collection? Information gathering through involvement with researchers (either individually or at a departmental level) is another useful tactic in developing data collections. It can be difficult to gather statistics on usage of digital collections as previously noted, so a needs assessment in the form of dialogue with researchers on what they are using or what they would like to obtain in the future can be used to measure current and potential demand. This can be combined with traditional subject consultancy work and departmental liaison in supporting research needs. In the analysis of a survey on existing digital data support carried out for the Association of Research Libraries it was noted, 'Consultation services such as identifying datasets, providing access to data, and articulating current standards for organization of data in specific subject areas seem to be a natural fit for subject librarians who provide similar services for other types of information' (Soehner, Steeves and Ward, 2010, 16).

Researcher liaison has the additional benefit of putting use of resources within a real world research context. Information may be gathered on not only what datasets or data resources are being used but also why they have been chosen. It may be that they represent the only available source of information on a subject or have a user interface that is popular, or integrates well with other tools. Alternatively, other researchers within a department or research centre might also use the resource and have developed an informal support group. A combination of user familiarity and word of mouth often plays a significant part in the take up of data resources. An appreciation of these qualitative factors can be just as important as usage statistics.

Requests for new datasets can also vary in importance and detail as far as readers are concerned. Some may be responding to some marketing material they have seen or a mention in an academic journal where they are curious about what is on offer. Others may have a detailed set of reasons that fit closely with a strong research need. Part of the data librarian's role is assessing new requests and liaising with the department to tease out these details in order to evaluate whether the need for a specific data collection is as strong as is suggested. As details about what is required become more apparent it may be that there are already datasets within your collection that would be just as useful to them. Alternatively, as further information is provided about how they intend to use data it can become clear that the dataset being requested is unsuitable for the intended purpose. All this illustrates how the interaction has value in educating you further as a data librarian about the needs of your researchers.

Refreshing and weeding a collection

Refreshing and removing items from collections can be an important stage of traditional library collection development and while it is perhaps not as time consuming within digital collections – especially as one is not dealing with physical items in most cases – it still has a place. The reasons for this can vary. Some data collections may be in formats that over time become obsolete and cannot be updated. Data suppliers may switch to new methods of dissemination, phase out older products or simply cease to exist. Resources are also not always as unique as some suppliers may suggest leading to the chance to swap and compare services. This is because

> Unlike books and periodicals, most data are not 'published', listed in catalogs of publishers, or even sold. Data collected by the U.S. government, for instance, [are] often available from multiple vendors since, for the most part, vendors can redistribute such data without having to pay the government royalties. This creates a situation where different vendors acquire the same data from the government, repackage the data differently, and then offer their product for sale or lease.
>
> (Geraci, Humphrey and Jacobs, 2012, 160)

Weeding a collection may also be the result of a conscious decision by the data librarian to add new products or to make better use of funds. Disposal of the resource may be necessary if a dataset is obtained on the basis of an ongoing subscription which no longer seems to provide good value for money. The resource may represent an ongoing cost but may have declined in popularity, seem to receive little use or simply be of less potential when compared with newer competing resources. Some diplomacy is needed in removing items from a collection as readers need to be consulted for their views on changes and a number of simple steps may be taken. The same communication channels that are used to gather opinion on new data resources could be used to assess the public impact of removing something. Other strategies include advertising in advance an intention to remove a data collection and inviting comment. If opinion received via e-mail, departmental meetings, blogs and so on is strongly against removal then this should be taken into consideration. This is another illustration of how these procedures can strengthen departmental liaison at many levels rather than just being about a data collection. It may still be possible to proceed in the face of opposition but strong reasons need to be demonstrated. Changes are easier if there is little interest expressed in a change but reasons should still be articulated.

Diminishing returns and safeguarding data

It would be a mistake to assume that collections need to be constantly assessed or refreshed in order to ensure that data are being acquired and attract high usage. This does not need to apply in every single case. There will be key datasets that are used frequently but these may in fact be in the minority. The Pareto Principle (Pareto, 1971), previously mentioned in Chapter 1, reminds us that most things have an unequal distribution and impact. So out of ten datasets perhaps only two or three will be the popular collections. It may be necessary to make decisions about allocating time, resources and effort based on this principle. In addition the value of some items in a collection may lie not in attracting high usage but rather in being unique, non-replicable or significant. They may also be significant assets that add additional flavour to a collection or are there to accommodate changes in research interests.

It is possible to take active steps in order to spark new interest in holdings rather than just responding to external changes. Collection development often involves identifying a percentage of datasets that can be held and curated in such a way as to attract greater usage. This can be done by highlighting them in promotional activities or by creating teaching materials around them. Additional documentation or curatorial activities such as expanded catalogue entries or the development of extended case studies make datasets more accessible and attractive to readers. Making them the subject of data visualizations, creating syntax files, if not available, marking them up for online analysis, or creating custom charts and infographics are further examples of how to cultivate new interest. One of the ideas behind the Pareto Principle can be summarized as the law of diminishing returns, which recognizes that selected key areas – rather than all areas – need to receive attention, time and effort. So one aim may be to make these selected data collections more usable and accessible.

Another area that often receives additional attention as part of collections development policy is the safeguarding of restricted data and monitoring compliance with restricted use agreements. Providing access to datasets that require additional protection is potentially a core activity of most data librarians and it will help define their role within a larger library setting. Formal policy and procedures need to be developed that promote the data librarian as the person to contact when restricted data are being sought or when help is needed in making applications. Most suppliers of restricted data – for example Statistics Canada, ICPSR, the Roper Center or Eurostat, which provide access to socio-economic data – require a specific person to be nominated within an organization and to provide an 'institutional signature'. At the University of Oxford, the LSE, European University Institute and elsewhere, it is the data librarian who is the nominee. Ensuring that one named person is responsible for confirming access restrictions are honoured is part of not only general research support, but also a deliberate policy of enabling restricted data collections to be added to current library holdings. It allows work to be done on promoting the availability of such data.

It also encourages researchers to think about their responsibilities when accessing and using data. Restricted access provisions can easily be overlooked by enthusiastic academics who are keen to get on with their research but the requirements of access agreements – or subscription licensing conditions – need to be stressed and enforced at all times. One of the responsibilities of the data librarian is to show they have taken reasonable steps to communicate this message. If data cannot be shared among departments or additional copies made for personal use this needs to be made clear. When access is granted but no rights to reproduce or amend tables is given such restrictions need to be communicated. It is not unknown for completion of dissertations to be delayed while cited – but unfortunately non-reproducible – content is removed. So where datasets have restrictions around their usage this needs to be properly explained to users.

Embedding data within the library

Library services have developed to respond to the demands of academics for support with open access publishing, providing access to digital resources and maintaining traditional support for discovery and use of books and journals. These rely on the library as a focus for this activity but the expertise embodied within it should not be overlooked as a vital ingredient. The importance of 'fields such as those of open access, copyright, metadata and archiving are evident. Less evident, but equally important, is the subject-specific knowledge of the different data collections. This is a prerequisite not only for the adequate description of data, but also for understanding the researchers' needs and the transformation of these into adequate technical solutions' (Kruse and Thestrup, 2014, 331).

There are also similarities in establishing obligations around the data being used with the traditional undertakings to which readers agree when joining a library. One of the goals of the Bodleian Data Library was to highlight the responsibilities users of data often sign up to but easily overlook (www.bodleian.ox.ac.uk/data/using-data/data-obligations). The UKDA makes use of an 'end-user licence' to outline these responsibilities that is five pages long (http://data-archive.ac.uk/media/381244/ukda137-enduserlicence.pdf). In a sense such concerns are not new. The rules around using books and collections at the original library of the University of Oxford – the Bodleian – are somewhat shorter. At their heart lies the original 'Bodley Oath' that is still in use,

Do fidem me nullum librum vel instrumentum aliamve quam rem ad bibliothecam pertinentem, vel ibi custodiae causa depositam, aut e bibliotheca sublaturum esse, aut foedaturum deformaturum aliove quo modo laesurum; item neque ignem nec flammam in bibliothecam inlaturum vel in ea accensurum, neque fumo nicotiano aliove quovis ibi usurum; item promitto me omnes leges ad bibliothecam Bodleianam attinentes semper observaturum esse.

I hereby undertake not to remove from the Library, nor to mark, deface, or injure in any way, any volume, document or other object belonging to it or in its custody; not to bring into the Library, or kindle therein, any fire or flame, and not to smoke in the Library; and I promise to obey all rules of the Library.
(www.bodleian.ox.ac.uk/about-us/policies/regulations)

The need to advocate appropriate use and prompt readers about their obligations applies to freely available government data, commercially purchased data, locally stored data, restricted access microdata and in fact anything promoted as part of a digital data collection. It also serves as a reminder that much of this data management activity and service development will overlap with that of the wider library – a process described as one of 'stepping in as a natural support for data related needs' (Levine, 2014, 143). Developing a data collection involves embedding it within the larger organization. This may already be occurring if earlier suggestions about using existing cataloguing and discovery mechanisms or filling holes in provision are pursued. Even in cases in which an academic library is only just beginning to consider digital research data as part of its collection policy the task of collection building and managing that collection ought to be seen as an exciting opportunity. As Sheila Corrall argues 'Libraries that are already involved in digital library developments, secondary data services and specialized research support are well positioned. . . . Libraries and librarians with less experience will have more to learn but much visibility, credibility and authority to gain on campus' (Corrall, 2012, p.127). Including digital collections could involve going further and seeing how data support can be placed in the context of other library activities. Existing support staff could be briefed on data collection policy and the work going on around it to make it more familiar to them. Opportunities for delivering additional training might also be pursued. Feedback and comment from doing this is also invaluable. If this work is seen as successful it will be another step in embedding and clarifying the role of the data librarian for data users and colleagues working within the library.

Key take-away points
- Management of digital data resources should be accommodated within library services.
- The data collection you cultivate will define your work, direction of future development and your support service.
- Data collections may consist of acquired physical copies or acquired access privileges.
- Techniques to inform selection of collections such as vendor trials, researcher recommendations and usage figures can help but may be inconclusive in themselves.
- The 'inside knowledge' of departmental interests provided by subject specialists can be central in making decisions.
- Collections need to be actively promoted using existing channels of communication or through new ones.
- Extensive data collections may necessarily have different access mechanisms rather than being available on demand.
- Changes to collections need to be managed in the same way as with traditional collections in order to maintain support of researchers.
- Facilitating access to sources of restricted data can be a core activity.

Reflective questions
1. Should you think in terms of a digital resource hotlist? What criteria would you use?
2. Are there data collections in use within departments which should more properly be held by the library?
3. What are the advantages and disadvantages of using access requests as a way of monitoring demand?
4. Is it better to steer a researcher towards a paid subscription resource or a free resource if the data are similar?
5. Are there key resources you need to include in your service that will help define it?
6. Do researchers have a clear path to follow to the library if they want advice on data or do they go to other various departments as well?

CHAPTER 5
Research data management service and policy: working across your institution

Librarians and RDM

Many data librarians working today are solo librarians or part of a small team. However, we would argue that for those data librarians who have become involved in work supporting research data management (RDM), working alone is not an option. There are too many components involved in institutional RDM support for one professional to be able to do it all. One parallel trend to employing data librarians in the UK is for academic libraries to hire an 'RDM services coordinator'. These may be the only full-time professional working on RDM, and their title recognizes the need to leverage input from service managers across the library and computing service, and beyond. In some cases these new posts have been based in the research office, rather than the library. In other cases support has been cobbled together from parts of people's jobs across libraries, research offices and IT departments. A DCC survey from 2015 found that 'At least two-thirds of [52 responding UK-based] institutions currently have less than 1 [full-time equivalent staff] allocated to RDM' with only those receiving the top third of research income expected to have more (almost three on average) by May 2016 (Whyte, 2015, 3).

For those without the luxury of being in a dedicated post, taking on data support is often a new job requirement from which none of the previous duties have been removed. While this may cause stress and even resentment for some, it really should be seen as an intellectual challenge and an opportunity to work with new researchers and colleagues outside one's normal circles. Even those in a dedicated data-related post who may be accustomed to serving a specific research community are being challenged to come out of their silos and combine forces with others across campus to join RDM committees and do some collective problem-solving. People skills or communication skills have never been more needed in the data support profession.

Similarly, it may be observed that there are two types of research institutions: those that embrace the RDM challenge proactively, and those that wait for funders' requirements to threaten research income or other external consequences (such as a scandal involving fraud, confidentiality breach or failure to comply with a freedom of information [FOI] request) before reluctantly taking action. If you find yourself in the first type of institution, consider yourself fortunate, as your efforts at self-education and outreach with new users will be supported and rewarded. But even if you are quite sure that you are in an institution with its head in the sand, take heart: this could be an opportunity for you (or the library) to demonstrate leadership by talking about the issues, getting people organized, and taking on pilot projects to establish evidence for the need for more resources for RDM support and services.

Institutional allies for RDM support

Leadership in RDM has sprung from different sources in different institutions. Much depends on the personalities, resources and strategic alignments at a given place and time. Although there is no single response to the RDM challenge, there is one thing that every successful response has in common: new allies and relationships are required by even the best prepared organizations. If the library takes the lead on RDM, it will need to seek the support of not only academic and administrative leaders but also support staff in other parts of the institution: IT, the research office, records management, data library (if not in the library) and research institutes. This has been a strong refrain in the chorus of institutional stories of RDM adoption, including this one from the University of Michigan:

> In academic libraries, a data management specialist may only interact with researchers at the beginning and end of a project, assisting with the creation of a data management plan (DMP) and preservation of the data when the research is completed. This poses a challenge when trying to help researchers integrate best practices into their workflows throughout the planning, collection, and analysis stages. . . . Given the diverse nature of research data and the distributed support researchers may seek throughout their project, universities need a well-connected, distributed way to support data management; it is a service that 'takes a village'.
>
> (Mohr, Johnston and Lindsay, 2016, 51)

The authors go on to explain the role of no fewer than 12 institutional players in the university's RDM infrastructure, as well as the close collaboration between the University Libraries and the College of Liberal Arts' Research Support Services, where the data librarian is based.

Why does an institution need an RDM policy?

Strategy, plan, roadmap, initiative, policy – these are all grand terms, especially when applied at an institutional level. Why has RDM suddenly become so important that research institutions, whether small, medium or large in size, seem to be falling over themselves in a rush to get themselves an RDM policy? The answer seems to be a combination of key top-down and bottom-up drivers.

Top-down drivers

First and foremost among the top-down drivers for institutional data policies are the research funders. Certainly in the USA and the UK, the most important government research funders, along with many other private and public funders, have been taking it in turns to issue new RDM requirements over the last five to ten years, and making granting of funds dependent on compliance, to a greater or lesser extent. There are three major reasons for this shift:

1. the pressures of the open access movement (with its message that publicly funded research should be made publicly available)
2. efficiency savings (avoiding paying two or more times for the same outcome of an experiment or project, especially where the result is not significant and goes unpublished)
3. accountability and prevention of fraud (being able to produce 'proof' of how conclusions were drawn).

More about these sorts of influences on science and scholarship can be found in Chapter 10.

The National Institutes of Health (NIH) was the earliest large funding agency to make waves on the western side of the Atlantic with its 2001 policy stating 'Data should be made as widely and freely available as possible while safeguarding the privacy of participants, and protecting confidential and proprietary data' (National Institutes of Health, 2003). Also, researchers submitting a funding application for $500,000 or more of direct costs in any single year to NIH are required to include a plan to explain how they will share their data, or explain why data sharing is not possible. Yet data management plans did not get the attention of institutions and libraries until the National Science Foundation in 2011 began requiring a two-page DMP with every application.

In 2013, the European Commission's Horizon 2020 research programme announced the Open Research Data Pilot, which mandated that projects applying to designated funding streams would be required to submit a DMP and to make their underlying data available in an open access repository. A peculiarity of the policy is that projects may opt out if they can show good cause, and projects from other strands may opt in if they choose, though participation does not improve their chances of being funded (European Commission, 2013).

Longstanding policies have also been developed by research councils which have a designated repository, such as the ESRC, which has been funding the UKDA under different guises since 1967. Recipients of grant funding for social science research have always been required to offer their data for deposit, though acceptance has depended on whether the dataset matches the archive's collection development policy. A small percentage of funds are held back from future funding applications if recipients are found to be non-compliant. (Though currently any enforcement with teeth from most funders is rare.) More recently, the ESRC updated its policy to allow deposit of data in any responsible digital repository as long as the UK Data Service, run primarily by UKDA, is notified of their location. (The repository must be considered FAIR: findable, accessible, interoperable and re-usable; see Chapter 7.) Similarly, the Natural and Environmental Research Council (NERC) funds a number of data centres for each of its disciplines: marine, atmospheric, earth observation, solar and space physic, terrestrial and freshwater, geoscience, polar and cryosphere) and partially funds the Archaeology Data Service.

None of the other UK research councils (known collectively as Research Councils UK (RCUK), but likely due in the near future to be consolidated into a single organization) followed their lead in setting up discipline-specific repositories. In fact, one of them, the Arts and Humanities Research Council, stopped funding their Arts and Humanities Data Service in April 2008, though it continues to fund one of the disciplinary repositories, the Archaeology Data Service. However RCUK did draft Common Principles on Research Data Policy, with a view to eventually agreeing a common policy (perhaps). The principles call for data to be made openly available with as few restrictions as possible in a 'timely and responsible manner', leaving the specifics to the individual funders or others to decide. Each of the seven research councils plus the Wellcome Trust (a private, charitable funder of biomedical research) has since issued or updated its own policy, each with slightly differing requirements as they grapple with providing practical guidelines. The subtlety of the differences has made the DCC's 'Overview of funders' data policies' web page essential reading for institutional data librarians, data managers and RDM co-ordinators (DCC, 2016).

Ironically, the last council to create a policy – the Engineering and Physical Sciences Research Council (EPSRC) – caused the most disruption to the sector by putting the onus of compliance on the entire institution, rather than the individual researcher. In doing this the EPSRC's 'Expectations' on institutions, forming part of its policy framework on research data, put an end to the passing of the football between the funders and the institutions as to the question of 'Who pays?' by spelling out 'clear expectations' that institutions should cover the costs of curation throughout the data lifecycle via its normal stream of funding (EPSRC, 2014). Most importantly, an RDM Roadmap was required to be put in place and then implemented by the very specific date of May 2015. All universities whose research funding includes a significant portion from EPSRC have not dared to ignore this edict. While a 'clear expectation' is in a sense oxymoronic and falls short of a clear *requirement*, institutions have chosen to treat it as the latter. Policies, roadmaps, new posts, services and training have come about for the majority primarily because of this perceived requirement. It is likely that other councils will emulate some of the EPSRC's expectations when updating their own policies. Indeed, the ESRC 2015 updated policy included institutional roles and responsibilities for the first time.

Bottom-up drivers

Of course there are a number of reasons an institution might want to have an RDM policy aside from the funders' mandates. It may help to spell out roles and responsibilities for data management that help meet other key institutional policies, such as information security, records management or research integrity. This has the added benefit of pitching these issues at a level to which most researchers or research teams will be responsive. Indeed, the University of Edinburgh's earlier adoption of the UK Research Integrity Office's Code of Practice for Research (http://ukrio.org/publications/code-of-practice-for-research) was one of the drivers – and justifications – for its own RDM policy. Another is the need to be able to respond to FOI requests about research effectively. This driver was brought to light by the 'Climategate' scandal at East Anglia University in 2009, in which the university administration was sanctioned by the Information Commissioner's Office for not responding to FOI requests about e-mails between researchers in a timely fashion. More importantly it had resulted in quite a lot of bad press for the university, which certainly got the attention of other UK university decision-makers.

The case study overleaf describes how a data audit led to a university policy.

Of course, research staff themselves may advocate for a policy to support them in achieving good practice. Alas, such altruism is relatively rare, hence the dominance of 'carrots and sticks' in the discourse about RDM policies. On the other hand, in our experience most academics will find themselves on

CASE STUDY How a data audit led to a university policy

One reason the University of Edinburgh passed its policy so early – May 2011, before the EPSRC requirements had come into play – was the recommendations from the Data Audit Framework (DAF, now Data Asset Framework) Implementation Pilot Project, conducted in 2008 by Information Services (IS) staff plus a handful of other institutions. This project, designed to test the effectiveness of the new DAF tool created by the DCC, conducted case studies in five departments, which consisted of data inventories and interviews with researchers and IT support staff. The results were a bit of a shock as they revealed not-so-good data management practice, but these were in line with the findings of other institutions (www.data-audit.eu/findings.html). In general, the findings showed:

- inadequate storage space (reliable, regularly backed up, secure, easily accessible)
- lack of awareness and understanding of research data management
- lack of formal research data management plans
- demand for training in research data management and curation
- lack of good practice guidance and advice from support services as and when needed
- lack of clarity about roles and responsibilities for research data management by university research staff.

The issue of storage space in particular was known, as it had been highlighted by a 2007 Research Computing Survey that IS had undertaken, in which researchers across disciplines wanted access to more centralized storage space. This was addressed in 2014 when a free 'half terabyte per researcher' of active data storage space that had been promised by then Vice Principal Jeff Haywood was procured, set up and rolled out across the institution as part of the RDM Programme.

The DAF work, which was overseen by a steering group that included academic data managers and researchers, the records management officer, a representative from the research office (Edinburgh Research and Innovation) and the university archivist had led to four major recommendations, which were followed up in future work. There should be:

- a university policy in research data management
- training for staff and postgraduates
- web page guidance on research data management
- a gap analysis of existing support services.

As proof of their commitment, the Steering Group chose to continue to meet after the project was over, and until the RDM policy and storage working groups were set up in 2010 by the Vice Principal. The four page report is available at http://edin.ac/22yceyk. The University of Edinburgh's Research Data Management Policy may be viewed at www.ed.ac.uk/is/research-data-policy.

common ground with respect to views on data management, given the chance to air initial opinions and concerns, as happens in a normal policy consultation process. This is 'because good research needs good data', as the tagline of the DCC home page currently states. Another reason for agreement on policy aims is that most researchers are eager to use other researcher's data, but reluctant to share their own. This is a frustrating paradox for data librarians, but perhaps is simply part of human nature.

What comprises a good RDM policy?

Our view is that an institutional policy needs to be clear and very readable, or else it will not be read and used. Hence the 'ten commandments' bullet point approach of the University of Edinburgh policy or the 12 points of the Policy on the Management of Research Data and Records of the University of Oxford. More detailed protocols and procedures should be developed and defined, but preferably at a lower level than institution-wide, as disciplinary practices and forms of data vary so much. The role of institutional policy is often to establish commitment to the services that will follow. When setting out actual content, it is most important to clarify roles and establish responsibilities, especially for individual researchers and the institution's services. A content analysis of UK institutional policies on the DCC website compares the existence or absence of content by such categories as definitions, support, DMPs, scope, ownership, external requirements, retention, ethics, access and costs. This analysis also considers whether the policy is subject to periodic review (Horton and DCC, 2016).

Tips for getting an RDM policy passed

It is very difficult to pass a policy without the buy-in of a senior figure. Look out for 'data champions' at every level of academic leadership and make sure they know you are an ally. Equally important is timing: has something happened within the university or in the wider world that makes an RDM policy particularly timely or untimely? In the UK, some institutions chose not to tackle the 'data issue' before making their submissions to the 2014 Research Excellence Framework (REF) – a very important national exercise that affects both individual careers and funding allocations to institutions. Be as informed and sympathetic as you can about the disciplinary-specific norms and pressures of research in your institution. Current examples of this are explored in Chapter 9. Are there strengths specific to your institution you can build on? Perhaps open access publication is already understood and practised widely among the staff, or there is a strong records management section, a data-intensive research facility, or a research support service such as a data library. Playing to these strengths can lend credibility to a policy push.

For further tips that take into account a number of experiences at UK institutions, we recommend the DCC case studies in *RDM Strategy: moving from plans to action* (Rans and Jones, 2013). If, after reading how others have achieved their aims you are wondering how you can make a start at your own institution, you could carry out an investigation using one of the toolkits described in the next section. The DCC operates a consultation service for institutions getting involved with or ramping up their RDM initiatives as well.

Toolkits for measuring institutional preparedness for RDM

If your institution is just beginning to engage with RDM, we suggest carrying out a fact-finding exercise using one of these toolkits. Each of these has been developed, tested and enhanced by RDM experts. You and your colleagues will need to invest some time to learn the methodology and find some academic guinea pigs with which to engage, but at the end of the process you will have a report to put on the agenda of relevant senior policy-making groups for their consideration. Not only that, you will feel much more grounded by collecting and analysing evidence arising from your own institution, and your confidence in talking about research and data management issues is very likely to increase.

DCC capability and maturity models (www.dcc.ac.uk/resources/tools-and-applications) are tools created by the DCC, building on their years of experience advising institutions on developing RDM services and policy. These include the capability model Research Infrastructure Self Evaluation (RISE), a framework to describe current and planned provision for ten service functions. Each function is described by three levels of capability: minimal compliance with research data policies, best practice applied to the institution's context, and provision of sector-leading practice for specialized needs. ReCap expands on these for data hosting and discovery functions (e.g. repositories), and can be used alongside the RISE model. Both models build on the earlier Collaborative Assessment of Research Data Infrastructure and Objectives (CARDIO) maturity model, which a number of UK universities have applied to benchmark how far their service has progressed from problem recognition through to an embedded service. The CARDIO is provided in several forms including a 'pulse check' quiz (http://cardio.dcc.ac.uk/quiz) to help organizations get started and a matrix to self-assess institutional progress towards compliance with research funder expectations.

The Data Asset Framework (www.data-audit.eu), also developed by the DCC, builds on records management appraisal methodologies to uncover the value of various data assets held by an organization. In practice, it has been modified to incorporate structured interviews with researchers as well. Brian Westra describes a use case at the University of Oregon, which used the tool to conduct a library needs assessment for data services for the sciences (Westra, 2010). More recently it was used at Georgia Tech (Rolando et al., 2013). A guide produced by the DCC and DataOne describes how 'DAF can fulfil an "intelligence gathering" role to inform CARDIO assessments, collecting evidence of researchers' current practices and views on service provision, which can then be used to re-assess the level of readiness these services have reached' (Whyte and Allard, 2014, 14).

Another approach has resulted in the Data Curation Profiles (DCP) Toolkit and DCP Lite (http://docs.lib.purdue.edu/dcptoolkit), both of which provide a framework for interviewing a researcher in any discipline about their research data and their data management practices. The original toolkit was developed by the Distributed Data Curation Center (D2C2) at Purdue University Libraries as part of an academic grant with a library school; its aim was to produce a body of comparable DCPs rather than to provide a tool for assessment of practice, making the documentation for conducting a profile rather extensive. DCP Lite followed this up and provides guidance for a short focused interview that could be conducted in one hour and without too much advanced preparation, with the intent of developing a solution or intervention. It is an example of how the general practice of interviewing is a tremendous confidence booster for librarians first dipping their toes into the data ocean. As an example, Anne Donnelly, Academic Liaison Librarian at the University of Edinburgh, discussed her feelings before and after conducting a data interview (http://datablog.is.ed.ac.uk/2013/09/18/first-data-curation-profile-created-at-edinburgh).

The Australian National Data Service (ANDS) Research Data Management Framework: Capability Maturity Guide (http://ands.org.au/guides/capability-maturity) is yet another approach to measuring institutional readiness for RDM. The ANDS adapted this from the Capability Maturity Model, originally applied to software development. Institutions are characterized by five levels of maturity from 'initial' to 'optimized' in four distinct areas: institutional policies and procedures, IT infrastructure, support services and managing metadata. These are presented in a grid, with each cell describing the nature of the service at this level, for example at level 4, 'managed': 'Metadata quality metrics collected. All datasets described & metadata shared.' At least one partial application of the framework was in University of Virginia's DM-Vitals methodology for interviewing researchers to assess a 'data management maturity level' (Sallans and Lake, 2014, 87–108).

These tools all show there is plenty of groundwork laid by others to alleviate the sense that you are starting from scratch for your own institution. Measuring the level of preparedness is vital in creating a foundation for future service developments.

Planning RDM services: what do they look like?

Setting up a new service is often quite an involved process. Often a business case must be presented, usually to those controlling the budget. Similarly, money for new services is difficult to locate and justify, especially in lean economic times, and difficult choices must sometimes be made about what other services and/or activities can be partially or fully defunded or retired to accommodate new ones. Even at the library staffing level, priorities about support for research over support for learning and teaching, and front-line support vs back-office collection management must be balanced before new services can be planned. Efficiency and value for money must ever be the watchwords for those interested in gaining funding for services.

Nevertheless, if an institution is interested in developing a new area, there are often seeds of ideas that can be nurtured, such as requirements-gathering evidence, pilot services demonstrating proof of concept, or deliverables from research and development projects that can be built on. All of these can feed into the business case to help demonstrate demand and just as importantly the means of provision.

Governance

Where money is involved, so is governance. As skills and infrastructure for RDM are often distributed rather than located in one department, this often leads to a truly cross-institutional governance committee, which can be very useful. Equally useful is to have stakeholders from the user community involved in the governance, either by leading or being members of some sort of steering group. Large institutions may require a board or steering group as well as a management group dealing with day-to-day operations. Currently the University of Oxford uses this two tier approach with a 'working group on research data' of senior management and RDM experts, which meets each term, and a more frequent 'delivery group' made up of RDM experts and library subject consultants.

The dangers of proceeding without proper governance include lack of sufficiently broad input from the researcher community to ensure services are fit for purpose, lack of academic buy-in for centralized services, and lack of uptake or demand for new services, any of which could be disastrous for continuation or increase of required funding. However, depending on the size of the enterprise envisaged, some good governance elements may be able to be incorporated without setting up an entire committee.

Lifecycle mapping and gap analysis

Two ways of planning or enhancing RDM services are best used together:

RESEARCH DATA MANAGEMENT SERVICE AND POLICY 77

research or data lifecycle mapping, and a gap analysis of existing services. A research lifecycle traces the activity of a researcher over the course of a research project; similarly a data lifecycle traces the path of the data, or the actions that are needed on the data to move the research to the next stage. A simple data lifecycle was shown in Chapter 2. The data lifecycle shown in Figure 5.1 is useful to show how services can be mapped onto a researcher-centred workflow.

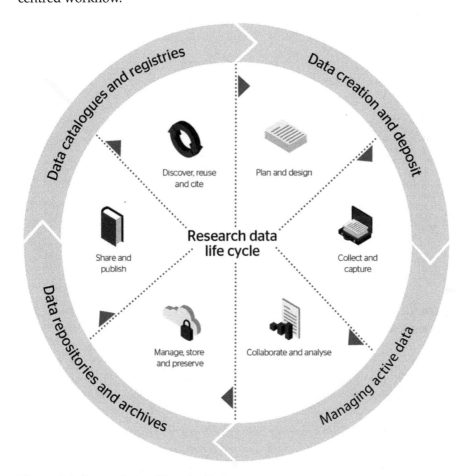

Figure 5.1 *Research data lifecycle diagram*
© Jisc, 2016 (www.jisc.ac.uk/guides/how-and-why-you-should-manage-your-research-data). Used with permission.

An advantage of a circular diagram is to show how the data continue to live on after the research project is over, albeit often in someone else's project. When data are shared – whether in an open or controlled way – any researcher across time and space may build on the dataset produced by one project as an *output*, and use it as an *input* to a new project, in either a predictable or completely new way. As Rufus Pollock, founder and President of Open Knowledge, has said, 'The coolest thing to do with your data will be thought of by someone else' (a variation of this quotation can be found at rufuspollock.org/misc).

Figure 5.2 shows how the University of Edinburgh RDM training programme, led by Dr Cuna Ekmekcioglu, uses the simple data lifecycle diagram from Chapter 2 (Figure 2.3, p.31) to train researchers about data management by breaking up their routine data management tasks into different parts of the lifecycle.

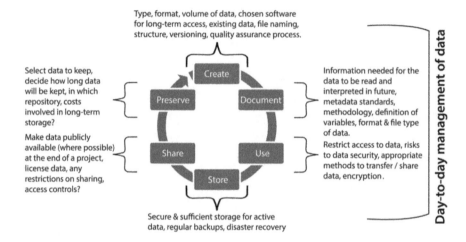

Figure 5.2 *Data lifecycle as used in good practice in RDM workshop*
© University of Edinburgh. Used with permission.

Academic support services can map existing services onto a lifecycle like the one shown in Figure 5.2 and then look for gaps in service. For example, on 'Create' there may be support for data management planning as part of research proposals. Or there may be a data discovery service to help researchers determine whether data already exist with a given set of parameters. For 'Document', there may be a metadata advisory service. 'Use' could include software support, statistical and GIS advice, training programmes, etc. 'Store' may mean a centralized, backed-up, secure file server either free at point of use or at cost, or a combination of the two (for example 'first X bytes are free'). 'Share' may mean the institutional repository, or it may be a service to help depositors find an appropriate repository in which to deposit their data, or both. 'Preserve' may be handled by the data repository, or it may be an individualized service that allows people to store files for the longer term without sharing. The latter requires policies to help the institution deal with the data after individuals leave, and it may also require metadata records about what the files contain for reasons of FOI or Data Protection Act requests.

Note that different data lifecycle models – there are lots of them – lead to different conclusions about the sorts of services that may be mapped on to them. Figure 5.3 gives an example of services mapped onto a data lifecycle model from Imperial College London.

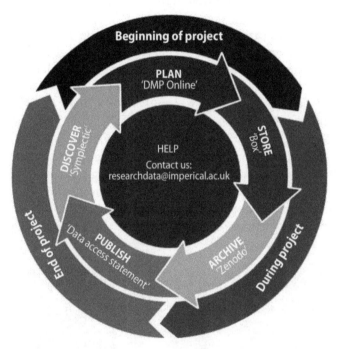

Figure 5.3 *Imperial College London Library RDM workflow, 2016*
Source: Ash Barnes (https://doi.org/10.5281/zenodo.54000 or https://zenodo.org/record/54000, CC-BY-4.0).

Edinburgh University's RDM Roadmap

The University of Edinburgh's RDM Roadmap (http://edin.ac/XnMS9E) (2012–2015, version 1.2 dated January 2014), authored by service managers in Information Services involved in RDM, used a data lifecycle mapping and a gap analysis to fill in high-level descriptions of enhancements of existing services and new services required to help implement the university's RDM policy (as well as the EPSRC expectations). It includes a number of objectives falling under four main categories:

- RDM planning: support and services for planning activities typically performed before research data are collected or created

80   THE DATA LIBRARIAN'S HANDBOOK

- active data infrastructure: facilities to store data actively used in current research projects and provide access to that storage, and tools to assist in working with and documenting the data
- data stewardship: tools and services to aid in the description, deposit and continuity of access to completed research data outputs
- data management support: awareness raising and advocacy, data management guidance and training.

While the first three categories reflect a very simple data lifecycle, or life course (before the research project begins, during the research project, and after the research project is finished), the fourth category underpins the entire process, empowering researchers to seek help or reskilling at whatever point they get stuck (see Figure 5.4). More recently (2015–16), the RDM Programme has been transformed into a single Research Data Service, which incorporates not only tools and support for RDM but also folds in other data-related services and training opportunities including Data Library & Consultancy, software preservation and guidance about working with cloud-based tools and research collaboration platforms. The goal is for the service to become a data solutions centre, where researchers can find help for any data-related issue they may be experiencing, or to reskill themselves in data management and use.

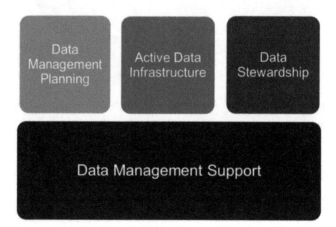

Figure 5.4 *University of Edinburgh's RDM Roadmap categories*
© *University of Edinburgh. Used with permission.*

Getting started

Sometimes the first thing a library does is create a new post and recruit to deal with the new RDM strategy. However it is both kinder on the new incumbent and more likely to be successful if some groundwork is laid first, if for no other reason than he or she may not have all of the hard and soft skills needed to set up a strategy and service that is necessarily transformative. By involving existing staff in early stages of RDM implementation, such as evidence gathering, professional development and awareness raising (or perhaps even training), the library can begin to create the internal culture change that is required for datasets not to be thought of as foreign objects by librarians, and for the data service not to become a silo, disconnected from other research and learning support services.

For example a lot of work was done at the University of Oxford in assessing researchers' needs and developing various data infrastructure services. This took the form of the Data Management Rollout (DaMaRo) at Oxford project. However a key role of the Bodleian Data Librarian was not only to help shape these services but also to promote them to other librarians and research support staff. Communication was important to keep colleagues informed of latest developments and create a sense that their views were feeding back into the overall process. DaMaRo was successful and laid the foundation for other services – with different names – which made communication even more important. This usually took the form of discussion workshops or training sessions aimed at increasing familiarity with the issues of RDM.

Before launching a brand new service it is wise to take small steps to gain confidence, learn from service users and fine-tune plans based on early experience. Piloting a support service with two or three friendly user groups is enormously helpful to determine if the service is fit for purpose in different disciplines, and can help gain allies and seed reputation through word of mouth. Of course there is no need to stick with known allies; one might pursue partnerships with trailblazer groups that are either sharing data already, or whose data are highly valuable. There are many ways to make a start usefully other than doing nothing.

Evaluation and benchmarking

Now that you have an RDM strategy, or at least the beginnings of one, it needs to be evaluated at every step of its implementation. By evaluation we mean a set of methods to measure the effectiveness or success of a service. Benchmarking is the comparison of one organization's success with others. Both are essential activities to determine whether a new RDM service or programme is on track. If you are reporting to a governance committee or a manager with overall responsibility for RDM services, you may have negotiated what is possible and informative to measure. If not, it is worth taking time out early on to think about what can be measured (readily or with some effort) and what evidence you will need to collect in order to show progress or success.

It can be difficult for pioneering institutions which have acted early to identify criteria for success. One important RDM activity to carry out is awareness raising, which is particularly hard to gauge. Librarians know that staff and students absorb information best at their own point of need, not at orientation and induction sessions, or at staff meetings. 'Why wasn't I told this service exists?' is a question service providers might have to get used to hearing, even from people who attended previous awareness raising sessions. Moreover, owing to the high turnover rate of postgraduate students and even staff at many institutions, it is not an activity that is ever easily marked off as completed. Formal and informal feedback at least can help you hone the message to make it more relevant and useful to busy academic researchers, or indeed to relocate delivery of the message to the researcher's point of need.

There are other evaluation methods. Website user testing methodology, including observation and task completion, can provide information about whether guidance pages or online services are working as they should. User surveys should be undertaken with care; they should be piloted for question understanding and usability, and best done on a sample rather than an entire population, to help improve response rates and reduce respondent burden. Be careful of raising expectations through implied future services in the questionnaire, and be sure to be clear whether you are describing existing services or potential ones. Focus groups and personal interviews are qualitative techniques for gathering feedback; reporting to a departmental meeting with time for Q&A can be equally illuminating, as well as convenient.

Where systems are in use, such as for storing or sharing data, uptake can easily be counted: how many logins, files, deposits, new collections, communities, gigabytes, users, downloads and so on, over time? There are any number of numerators to count usefully; the tricky part is determining the appropriate denominators. If one-third of a new petabyte store is filled within a couple of months is that a good or bad rate of uptake? If three-quarters of departments have created collections in an open data repository after the first year is that good or bad? Is it more important to get all the departments using it or to get more collections from existing departments? Does 30 downloads in a month mean a dataset is popular? If three principal investigators have sought advice from the library about a DMP for a research proposal in a month, is that a good rate of uptake? How many others have written plans without consulting the library or IT service; does it matter? How well are referrals working; are there gaps in the referral network? How many researchers or research groups are following and updating their plans after they receive funding? These are questions each institution needs to grapple with for themselves.

Benchmarking can help ease anxieties by comparing one's nascent RDM services with other similar organizations. A number of RDM institutional case studies have been written, which can provide qualitative comparisons, but surveys like the DCC's 2014 RDM Survey are an important benchmark of the sort that we will require more of as time goes on (e.g. see Figure 5.5).

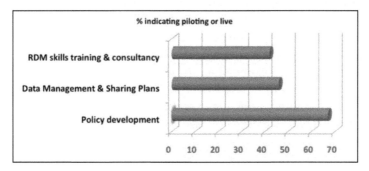

Figure 5.5 *RDM services in place, DCC 2014 RDM Strategy to Action Survey*

Source: Angus Whyte, blog post (www.dcc.ac.uk/blog/rdm-strategy-action-glass-half-full). There were 87 respondents at 61 UK institutions including all 24 from the Russell Group.

Standards can help with benchmarking your services, where they exist. For example, if your institutional repository is COUNTER-compliant (www.projectcounter.org), you can compare certain repository statistics against others, such as the number of downloads. The IRUS-UK service (www.irus.mimas.ac.uk) allows comparisons by data type (such as 'dataset'), and is piloting special views on data repositories (e.g. taking into account the numerous files that can be downloaded in a single dataset).

What is the library's role?

A number of library organizations from various countries have published reports about the need for academic libraries to get involved with data support to secure their future relevance to the scholarly record and science. An excellent list that has not dated too quickly was compiled by an e-science working group of LIBER, the Association of European Research Libraries – *Ten Recommendations for Libraries to Get Started with Research Data Management* (Christensen-Dalsgaard et al., 2012).

The League of European Research Universities (LERU) developed a Roadmap for Research Data in 2013 which took a broader view of RDM and the institution's role. Research libraries were key informers and contributors. The roadmap considered challenges posed by RDM under the following headings: policy and leadership; advocacy; selection and collection, curation, description, citation, legal issues; research data infrastructure; costs; and roles, responsibilities and skills (LERU, 2013). They are following this activity up with the LEARN project (http://learn-rdm.eu; 2015–17), which aims to offer a model RDM policy and a toolkit to support implementation, with dissemination in several languages.

As mentioned above, your library may be a leader in developing new RDM services, or it may be more of a secondary player. Whether you work in a large central academic library, a site or departmental library, or a data library, you and your colleagues are better off thinking through what role you wish to play rather than letting some other actor decide for you. Will the librarians be the public face of the service, consulting researchers about data management planning, referring them to other experts as needed? Should they act as trainers, augmenting existing roles in information literacy? Will they work closely with researchers in determining their sharing strategy by giving advice on IPR and licensing? Could they use their traditional library skills and actively advise on discovery metadata and domain-specific metadata schemas? Will they experiment with charging structures for in-depth support, or even direct costing from grant proposals? Is there an option for librarians to provide assistance in depositing data into the university repository or elsewhere? Will they take responsibility for the long-term preservation of academic data assets, or for open and closed datasets? The answers will depend on resources, staff talent and initiative, nature of existing services and, in the last instance, the inclination, drive and determination of library and/or other institutional leaders.

Key take-away points

➤ Even though many institutions have only one RDM post, many service contributors are generally needed.
➤ Funders have been the strongest driver for the development of institutional RDM policies.
➤ A common requirement from funders is the submission of a DMP, usually as part of the research proposal.
➤ Less common is the requirement to deposit resulting data in a designated repository, though sharing data in some way tends to be required unless reasons not to can be demonstrated.
➤ A good institutional data management policy establishes roles and responsibilities at a high level, allowing protocols and particular behaviour to be developed at levels that can take (changing) disciplinary norms and standards into account.
➤ Governance is an essential part of service development, preferably with academic input.
➤ A data lifecycle model is useful for mapping data services to research workflows, and discovering gaps. It should be used with care in communicating services to researchers; it may be more appropriate for

training purposes, when researchers have time to reflect on its meaning for them.
➤ A number of toolkits have been created to help institutional representatives decide how to establish or evaluate their RDM services.
➤ Evaluation refers to a set of methods to measure the effectiveness or success of a service. Benchmarking is the comparison of one organization's success with others. Approaches to both are needed to help you understand if your data services are on track.

Reflective questions

1. Why are soft (people) skills important in developing and delivering research data services?
2. Are you familiar with the RDM policies of the funders your research community relies on?
3. If your institution has a RDM policy, how is it communicated to researchers? Do you think they are aware of it? Are open access (publication) policies better understood?
4. Rather than wait for a top-down policy, champion or funds, what might you be able to do straight away to improve RDM practice at your institution or department?
5. How important do you think it is for libraries to be leaders in RDM support?

CHAPTER 6
Data management plans as a calling card

Responding to challenges in data support

Academic librarians play an important role in supporting the research process throughout its many phases. In order to maintain this level of support they also need to be responsive to new requirements being placed on researchers. So while there are expectations from institutions and funders that more thought be given to the general principles of data management, there are also specific stages in the data lifecycle where new and potentially unfamiliar activities may be identified and supported. The production of a DMP is a perfect example of such an activity. It is an important stage in the management of research data where, 'Principal investigators (PIs) . . . document their plans for describing, storing, securing, sharing, and preserving their research data' (Bishoff and Johnston, 2015, 1), but also presents an opportunity for academic librarians to give guidance and introduce themselves to their target audience. Preparation of a DMP benefits from various stages of redrafting much like a consent agreement (a document discussed within this chapter and in more detail in Chapter 8). It is an opportunity for the data librarian to offer support and advice for what is becoming a key document – but also one that may be unfamiliar even to experienced researchers – which will have a great deal of impact.

Leading by example: eight vignettes

In this chapter we have selected case studies – or vignettes – from a range of disciplines to show how the demands of RDM are being dealt with at different institutions and how advice on data management planning is being used to establish links and recognition. Each is written by a different data librarian, research data manager or data professional, and illustrates how the needs of researchers are addressed through a mixture of awareness raising about RDM and troubleshooting specific details of project administration.

Social science research at the London School of Economics and Political Science

Laurence Horton, Data Librarian, Digital Library, London School of Economics

Before the LSE Library set up an RDM support service in 2014, data management planning support consisted of the research office providing award applicants with a plan from someone's previously successful application and letting them copy and adapt it.

Since the LSE Library set up its RDM support service, grant application managers have either referred researchers to the library or approached the library on behalf of researchers. Thanks to promotion efforts and activities like our web pages, fortnightly open question sessions, and 'Writing a DMP' training, researchers are now contacting the service independently with their RDM queries – although most DMP inquiries still come through referral from the research office.

From October 2016 LSE requires all researchers with funded projects to have a DMP. In anticipation LSE Library has adapted DMPonline (https://dmponline.dcc.ac.uk) with customized LSE specific support for funder templates plus our own templates for Master's and undergraduate student theses and dissertations. In association with a data supplier, we also introduced a rule to write a plan to access one of our data resources.

Being a social-science-focused institution LSE receives a lot of ESRC funding and produces mostly social science data. Reflecting this, I run training on writing plans using DMPonline built around ESRC or Horizon 2020 (European Commission) requirements. These sessions also include an introduction to the UK Data Service's ReShare and the European Commission's Zenodo repositories as platforms for depositing research data.

Reviewing DMPs gives us an ongoing education in information security (data storage and back-up practices and infrastructure), law (data protection, FOI and intellectual property), librarianship (collections, organization, metadata) and archiving (file formats, size).

For difficult cases, I can find support from various people and organizations. LSE has specialists in information security, research ethics, data protection and FOI law, copyright and research methodology, and, of course, a good library team. Also, a great external community offers formal or informal support through organizations like the DCC, UK Data Service and other data archives, the Jiscmail-hosted RDM list, IASSIST and the RDA.

The LSE RDM support service sees the library taking the initiative in the

School to support researchers. The hope is, and early signs are, that as we meet initial needs so the demand for support within the school will grow.

This approach demonstrates the need to develop a support framework that is characteristic of the host institution. In this case a deliberate choice is made to tie RDM support in with not only particular funding bodies but also specific funding programmes. Regular training or consultation sessions are also used to focus support on researchers' plans where relevant to the application stage of a project and for their execution and completion. Making production of a DMP a pre-condition of accessing some key data collections is another interesting innovation that capitalizes on the role of the library in supplying data as well as advising on its management.

Clinical medical research at the London School of Hygiene and Tropical Medicine

Gareth Knight, Data Manager, Library and Archive Services, LSHTM

Anna Karenina never wrote a DMP, but the principle that success is not due to a particular positive trait but rather the avoidance of any number of negative ones certainly applies when providing data management support. For every plan that meets all funders' requirements, there are ten with data management issues that are challenging in their own way. In some cases, this is simply a matter of helping researchers to transfer their ideas to a written document, while other cases require more specific guidance on data handling practice.

For a university specializing in global health research, with a large clinical trials unit, primary data management concerns relate to how personal and sensitive data associated with research participants are handled. Studies must comply with data protection legislation, the International Council for Harmonisation Good Clinical Practice standard and other relevant regulations, even when working in countries that do not have specific requirements in this area. This requires consideration of data handling practices performed at every stage of the research process.

First, consideration must be given to how data are collected. Social surveys and medical assessments have traditionally been performed using paper forms. However, it is increasingly common for studies to use mobile devices, such as phones and tablets. These devices offer many advantages over paper-based collection, enabling the introduction of automated quality checks and avoiding the need for time-consuming data entry activities. However, they can be challenging to use, particularly when performing research in developing countries. It is common for researchers to request advice on the hardware and software that they should use, as well as the likely costs of purchase and import fees when writing research bids. Further discussion during a project's planning phase will explore the practicalities of their use in the field: procedures necessary to ensure devices are regularly charged in locations where electric generators are operated for just a few hours each day, and data synchronization methods to be applied in places with limited telephone and internet access. Thought will also be given to how they can resolve problems that may arise, such as the use of paper forms in scenarios where mobile devices cannot be used.

Second, information security practices to be applied during the study must be considered. This covers physical security methods, such as use of locked and managed facilities, as well as digital security techniques, such as use of encryption and access controls. It is common for researchers to get in touch on multiple occasions to enquire about security measures; in the initial stages to request an overview of the different options available and later to request training on a specific tool or an update on current practice. For instance, researchers who have encrypted their laptop may require advice on the practicalities of securing a phone, tablet or audio recording device.

Finally, it is necessary to consider how the requirements to protect study participants will be balanced with obligations to make data available. This is a multifaceted issue that requires a combination of technical, legal and domain expertise to address. In the first instance, it is necessary to determine the feasibility of making data available, by reviewing the data's content and consent forms signed by study participants. Direct identifiers, such as names and location details, which can be used to identify an individual in isolation, are easy to recognize. However, assessing the likelihood that values can be combined to re-identify an individual is problematic, particularly if the information is held in a separate dataset. In these cases, domain expertise may be required to identify previous studies and resources that have covered the same study population. At the same time, the consent agreements should be reviewed to determine permissions provided. In cases where data sharing has not been considered (which remains common for long-running studies), it will be necessary to seek advice from the institution's ethics committee on the feasibility of making data available and any associated conditions. If data can be anonymized and made available to all, they may be uploaded to a research data repository. Otherwise, restrictions may be necessary, such as requiring users to register their interest and sign a legal agreement before being provided with data for analysis.

Data management plays a key role in health research, ensuring that researchers comply with a variety of legal, regulatory and ethical obligations. However, it must not be considered simply a box-ticking exercise to meet third party requirements; careful planning of data management activities is intrinsic to ensuring research is performed in a manner that protects study participants and enables research goals to be met.

This approach shows the value of data management planning as an activity that covers the whole of the research process. The data professionals in this case are clearly conscious not only of the fact that live participants are involved but also that they need to offer advice and guidance within a pre-existing legal and ethical framework. This results in a concern with the fine details of how the research will be conducted and in how the aspirations of security and ethical practice discussed at the application stage will be carried into practice in the field.

Archaeological research at the University of California, Los Angeles
Deidre Whitmore, Manager, Digital Lab & Digital Publications, UCLA Cotsen Institute of Archaeology
Libbie Stephenson, Director, UCLA Social Science Data Archive

The Rock Art Archive (RAA) holds a set of private collections of papers, research reports, site reports, correspondence, journals, books and book galleys, videos, audiotapes, films, tracings on plastic and fabric, and photographic and slide images of rock and cave pictographs and petroglyphs (rock art). These collections, in some cases, constitute the only extant record of sites that no longer exist. Historically, some subfields within archaeology perceived rock art as a non-tangible artefact and any mention of rock art in conjunction with the study of an archaeological site would be in footnotes. The archaeological value of rock art has increasingly been recognized and now the study of rock art is deemed its own field or sub-discipline. Research on rock art is conducted internationally and in a variety of contexts. The archive was established to support and preserve donated collections from rock art researchers and avocationals. Staffing consists of the director, work study students and volunteers.

Three main databases were created to store and maintain information about the collections: an archive master database, correspondence and a special collections catalogue. The databases contain metadata describing each item in a collection and are updated regularly. There are 15 special collections and 14 assorted collections of major value. Materials are organized by category: reference materials, site records, special collections, visual materials and educational materials. Numerous publications have resulted from materials archived at the RAA.

In response to a report prepared by the RAA for their five-year interdepartmental review, the staff sought assistance to develop a DMP. The comprehensive review of the RAA holdings and systems for this report revealed issues the RAA staff wanted to address. In particular, copyright and intellectual property issues affected items within the collections. As a result of the DMP, the team developed a donor agreement form and retroactively contacted all previous donors to secure and document a rights agreement. An additional process was developed for researchers wishing to use the collections.

Because many items in the collection were being digitized, the DMP process provided an opportunity to consider the ramifications of building and sharing a digital collection. In order to proceed, we first carried out a DCP, as specified by Purdue University Libraries. In addition to the DCP, we also used the information on DMPs offered by the California Digital Library and by ICPSR. The team also researched discipline-specific repositories such as Open Context, the Digital Archaeological Record (tDAR) and Archaeology Data Service (ADS).

Part of the work focused on considerations for the stakeholders in the Rock Art Community – government agencies, cultural heritage organizations, property owners, avocationals and researchers and funding agencies. Owing to threats of vandalism, human impact, theft and cultural values, it is a commonly accepted practice to restrict access to geographic location information. Therefore, a process whereby scholarship could take place had to be factored into the planning.

The work considered requirements for the long-term preservation of digital images from two perspectives; bit stream preservation and functional preservation. Bit stream preservation has to do with ensuring that the bits comprising an image are not damaged, lost or corrupted. Functional preservation concerns those activities which are used to describe, provide access to, and maintain usability regardless of changes in hardware or software technologies. This approach was helpful because RAA had primarily been focused on analogue conservation and the process of digitization itself. In consideration of their needs for long-term preservation and dissemination, and the extent and scope of metadata requirements, the team decided that building an in-house repository which would follow best practices was preferable to locating the data within one of the existing repositories.

The RAA staff was enthusiastic about carrying out a DCP and, in turn, other researchers at the Cotsen Institute of Archaeology began to consider similar conservation measures. An additional DMP involving reflectance transformation imaging and archaeological sites and/or artefacts was prepared for another researcher at Cotsen. The DMP was a logical outcome of the DCP and was useful in communicating about the RAA with administration and funders. The services provided helped the RAA staff to understand the link between their work and information management, and the need for personnel with information studies and data management expertise as part of a sustainable operation. In fact, one staff member decided to obtain a graduate degree in the field of information studies as a result of working on this project.

Over the course of our consultations it became clear that the terminology used in conservation and rock art descriptions, as well as the language of curation and preservation, would need to be defined for everyone to proceed. Discussions frequently involved coming to an understanding about meaning and context. Reviewing the resources available on the websites of other repositories, such as tDAR and ADS, was helpful in developing an understanding of the field and associated terminology.

As a result of the work on the DCPs and DMPs the RAA is producing an online handbook and guide to its holdings. Additionally, we continue to be in contact as the RAA staff prepares a grant to fund the next steps. Our time with the RAA directly benefited our work as a data archivist and aspiring data manager. It enriched our knowledge about the field and expanded our thinking about data management planning and preservation. We will miss not being able to continue to meet this team and being a part of their work going forward.

This vignette from UCLA shows the many benefits that data management planning can have for an emerging discipline. The academic study of rock art is described as a once ephemeral branch of archaeology that is now becoming more substantial. This is a process that is helped immeasurably by a planned approach to data sharing, confidentiality, copyright, intellectual property issues and digital preservation. These are typical issues for data management but the discipline also takes some of them in unusual directions. Access controls are needed but these are to prevent disclosure of information not about individuals but of geographical locations.

These accounts describe the process of moving beyond simply promoting the need for RDM, to actually demonstrating in practical terms the usefulness of data management planning in more effectively conducting current and future research projects. The closing comment about the benefits of this process to those offering advice and support is also noteworthy. This thought is in fact a common one and emerges in other vignettes.

Geological research at the University of Oregon
Brian Westra, Science Data Services Librarian, University of Oregon
As part of the development of RDM services, the libraries have built and maintained a collaborative relationship with grant administrators and pre-award staff in the Office of Research. One of the outcomes is that they have been proactive in directing faculty to us for data management issues. In this case, they referred a professor in geology to me. This researcher was working on a National Science Foundation (NSF) Arctic natural sciences research funding proposal, and it was his first attempt at writing a DMP. He contacted me about a week prior to the proposal deadline, which is not uncommon.

The NSF Arctic Sciences Section included their policy on sharing scientific data in the program solicitation. The policy outlined the requirement that data and associated metadata must be deposited in an appropriate open access archive. Further, it required that metadata for discovery should be deposited in the Advanced Co-operative Arctic Data and Information Service (ACADIS) Arctic Data Repository, and described some of the types of metadata that should be provided. Some research domains are still developing infrastructure and best practices, and the variability in discipline-specific NSF guidance is a conscious and deliberate reflection of this.

However, it cannot be emphasized enough how helpful a greater level of detail is for proposal authors and those of us who support them. When funder guidance makes note of a functional, relevant data repository, even as a representative example, it removes some of the ambiguity that is often a barrier to good data management planning. The reference to ACADIS provided an avenue for the researcher to explore and understand the repository structure, data deposit process and application of the catalogue of metadata records to finding, understanding and using data. Given that I consult across many different science subjects, this was also an opportunity for me to become more familiar with this resource and the particular requirements for Arctic sciences.

We prioritize the use of national data centres and sustainably funded open domain repositories over the use of our institutional repository, but in some cases no compelling alternative exists. The researcher was planning to deposit the project data into our institutional repository, and this was reflected in the final plan.

As is sometimes the case, the proposal budget did not account for data curation costs, but this was not an issue since the professor projected that the amount of data would fall below the threshold at which the library usually charges a fee. Eventually we hope to develop a clearer cost structure for data curation infrastructure, but we are not alone in this regard. His first draft of a plan was based on information from our website, which outlines the common components and best practices for an NSF DMP. I reviewed his draft and the NSF guidance with him, and shared an example from another faculty member for a geosciences proposal. Although it was for a different NSF division, it was a robust exemplar of the structure and components of a good DMP.

The end result was a well written plan, but unfortunately the proposal was not awarded funding. A positive outcome in the form of a good plan, however, has resulted in several subsequent DMP consultations for proposals to other directorates. In this case and several others, consultations have also opened the door to checking in with the researcher about data curation for his current projects, and offers of help with data deposit in our repository when the time comes.

This story shows how offering advice on general or detailed funder requirements is a regular task and one which improves researcher confidence in planning for preservation and sharing. It also illustrates how this interaction can be an opportunity for the data professional to reflect on the services being developed and offered by the library. In this case the usefulness of a collaborative relationship established between the office of research and the library and the effectiveness of data repository services could be considered.

Medical and veterinary research at the University of Glasgow
Mary Donaldson, Research Data Management Officer, Library and Collection Services, University of Glasgow

This request for help came about because the research manager at the Centre for Virus Research had attended a presentation we had given on data management and was aware of the DMP review service we were offering.

The Centre had to prepare a DMP as part of its quinquennial funding review for the Medical Research Council (MRC). This block of funding supports eight major research programmes within the centre and initially there were two options for writing the DMP – eight individual DMPs or one overarching DMP. Some of the programmes were part of wider multi-partner collaborations; others conducted research that required ethical approval.

We proposed (to avoid repetition and duplication of effort) that each principal investigator would write a DMP which covered the sections of the MRC template that corresponded specifically to their own research programme. The director of the Centre would write an overarching DMP which covered the remaining sections, where there was a commonality of approach (sections on data security, data sharing and access, responsibilities and relevant policies). This approach was proposed to the MRC and deemed to be acceptable. There was one research programme that was sufficiently different in terms of the type and scale of the data that it required its own separate DMP.

Each principal investigator was allocated time with a member of the Data Management Service. They were introduced to DMPonline, our institutional data repository (which was relatively new at the time), and had the opportunity to discuss the content of their DMP. We also offered to review the plans once they had been drafted and give constructive feedback. The director was also supported in the production of the overarching DMP and boilerplate text was provided about the institutional data repository.

We have recently heard that the funding application was successful and the Centre has received funding for a further five years. Many of the principal investigators involved have commented that the time with the RDM service was extremely valuable and writing their DMPs (which they were uncertain about), had become one of the more straightforward parts of the quinquennial review application.

The only feedback on the DMP from the reviewers of the application was on standardization of methods and protocols across the research programmes, rather than on the DMP itself.

Working directly with the researchers in the Centre allowed us to spread the message about the Data Management Service and the services we offer to a wider audience than we had reached previously. Since then, some of the researchers from the Centre have attended RDM training courses we offer and others have deposited data in the institutional repository. We consider that positive interactions like these create 'data management champions' who are more likely to spread the word to their colleagues, in turn helping us reach more researchers. This should drive future demand for our services.

Astronomical research at Columbia University

Amy Nurnberger, Research Data Manager, Columbia University Libraries
'Ring, ring . . . ring, ring' is how many of these exchanges start. I know, 'The phone? Who calls anymore?' People who have a quickly approaching deadline and do not have the time for e-mail turn-around, that's who uses the phone. This particular researcher was directed to the university RDM Programme by our Office of Research's director of research initiatives and collaborations. The researcher was looking for review and guidance on a DMP for an astronomy project that would produce sky maps based on instrument-generated data kept in a time-ordered data archive. In common with many astronomy projects, the total amount of expected data was . . . large, ~100 terabytes (TB). As the saying (about money) goes, a TB here, a TB there, pretty soon, you are talking about real data!

Fortunately, the field of astronomy has an established history of well developed data file format standards that are widely recognized and employed in the discipline, such as FITS (Flexible Image Transport System), NetCDF4 (Scientific Data Network Common Data Format), and HEALPix (Hierarchical Equal Area isoLatitude Pixelization), so data format issues were not a concern. Equally well established in the discipline is the use of the pre-print server arXiv (arXiv.org), which provides a publicly accessible outlet for the products of astronomical research. Given astronomy's history of producing massive amounts of data, there are also robust data-sharing platforms available to researchers, such as those hosted by the US National Aeronautics and Space Administration, and strong cultural expectations for their use. The researcher clearly stated the intention of the project to fulfil those data-sharing expectations by taking advantage of the available disciplinary resources within a defined timeframe.

Although the discipline has a strong foundation in data sharing with acknowledged disciplinary practices, I assisted with the development of the DMP by encouraging the researcher to think through project-specific issues. These issues included clarifying distinctive data products and their respective qualities, detailing data documentation practices, providing contact information for unpublished data, and contingency planning for data care and safekeeping in the case of researchers moving to a different institution. One general area I was able to influence was to recommend the use of data citation for better attribution, provenance and re-use tracking (Martone, 2014). Most of these issues and their solutions are not specific to a discipline (the caveat being specific implementations of data descriptors and metadata, as opposed to the general principle of employing them). Recognizing that issues like these are common across disciplines is a powerful realization that can allow data management programs with restricted resources to work effectively with researchers across the institution without necessarily having in-depth disciplinary familiarity.

My perspective on partnering with researchers on data management planning is that they are the experts in their discipline, on their project, and with their data, and I am the expert on RDM – its principles, practices and available resources. I had the opportunity in this case to introduce considerations and practices that will ultimately contribute to developing a stronger research data re-use ecosystem. However, it was not appropriate to direct the researcher to local resources because of the nature of the project and the data. Regardless of the final funding decision on this project this exchange afforded an occasion for me to learn more about the work, data and practices in this area of astronomy, and for the researcher to build on fixed disciplinary practices in ways that could aid future data re-use and research reproducibility.

The previous two vignettes are good examples of how offering advice on writing DMPs can act as a bridge and create fruitful working arrangements with departments. In the case of the University of Glasgow opportunities for streamlining processes and removing duplication are recognized and taken. Researchers felt uncertain about what was required from them and appreciated the guidance they were given. The discipline at Columbia University had a much stronger tradition of data sharing and standardization of file formats. Even so, there were still enough unfamiliar areas regarding data curation and citation to ensure the advice was eagerly received.

Engineering research at the University of Guelph
Carol Perry, Associate Librarian, Research Enterprise & Scholarly Communication, McLaughlin Library, University of Guelph
The University of Guelph has been intrinsically involved over a couple of

years in the development of a Canadian national online bilingual DMP tool, DMP Assistant (http://assistant.portagenetwork.ca/en (the English language page), based on the DCC DMPonline tool.

Locally, we have prepared for the upcoming Canadian Tri-Agency funding council's DMP requirement and their recent open access policy on publications (including a data deposit requirement) by creating online guides and support materials covering all aspects of data management throughout the research lifecycle. Our data repository service is fully developed in preparation for increased requests for depositing data. We have been working closely with our Office of Research over the past two years to deliver information sessions and workshops to faculty and graduate students related to DMPs and open access requirements.

The development of an RDM service at the University of Guelph Library in 2009 provided a new suite of support services previously unavailable at our institution.

In 2010, following an outreach presentation to the various colleges, we were contacted by a research group leading a long-running multi-institutional research project. They realized that without a coherent mechanism for managing, storing and preserving data, the risk of potential data loss would increase over time. This was our first large-scale project management request.

We began by interviewing the project lead and a number of research support staff within the area. It was important to document their concerns and to discuss their current workflows. From these discussions, we developed a questionnaire in order to conduct a data audit based on criteria from the DCC's Data Asset Framework (www.data-audit.eu). On reviewing the results, we identified the areas of risk for the project and assessed the levels of risk associated with the findings.

We provided the group with a preliminary report highlighting our findings in a number of areas. After reviewing the report and determining potential solutions in consultation with the lead researcher, we produced a final report with a series of recommendations complete with deliverables, target dates for solutions as well as identifying options for where implementation responsibilities should rest.

This research group was very supportive of our work and immediately began implementing the most critical areas of concern. Some of the solutions, such as digitizing print-based manuals and other documentation, establishing new folder and file naming conventions and access controls, and establishing protocols for describing data assets, were easy solutions that could be implemented by support staff over time. Dealing with file migration issues and movement of their database to a client–server platform for multiple institutional access required significant resources, which the research group was committed to undertaking.

This experience was highly gratifying. It highlighted the importance of sharing knowledge and techniques internationally through documentation such as the DCC manuals as well as training opportunities to acquire the skills necessary to complete such an audit.

Although many of the audits undertaken since that time have been smaller in scope, this project gave us the confidence to know we possessed the skills to dramatically improve the long-term viability of an important research project.

Health-related social science research at the University of Bath
Alex Ball, Research Data Librarian
Catherine Pink, Senior Data Librarian
Lizz Jennings, Technical Data Officer, University of Bath

The University of Bath Library offers several services to researchers, including a Research Data Service (RDS). When promoting this service in departmental meetings, inductions and training sessions, we give out the e-mail address of the RDS request tracker and encourage researchers to use it for any enquiries related to RDM, including requests to discuss requirements or to have their DMPs checked prior to submission.

We received a request from a researcher in the Department for Health who wanted to discuss a proposal to use digital technology for community engagement. After meeting the researcher we learned that the project would try to assemble qualitative data about the physical activity of participants using a variety of techniques, including recordings of interviews and discussions, and a digital bricolage of photographs and narratives created by participants.

Our first priority was to understand with greater clarity what the research would actually involve. We did not have specialist knowledge of the field so we had to discuss some of the terms with the researcher, such as 'participatory action research' and, indeed, 'digital bricolage'. The latter transpired to be, in this instance, a website where participants would contribute photographs they had taken and narratives they had written, and work with the researchers to create an impression of their home town.

Our next step was to identify the data management issues that the researcher would have to tackle. One major concern was the area of data protection, privacy and consent. We pointed out some of the ways privacy can be compromised accidentally and techniques for avoiding them: blurring images, stripping out metadata embedded in audio files and digital photographs, transcribing recordings, and so on. We also provided recommendations on what should be included in the consent forms – for example, permissions to retain and share anonymized data, agreement on what will be kept and what redacted, and agreement on whether certain data could be shared in a restricted fashion without being fully anonymized – and suggested that the researcher also consult the University's data protection team. We encouraged the researcher to consider the risk that participants might compromise others' privacy in the photographs they took; as a result, the researcher planned to cover this issue when training participants, and in an additional quality assurance check.

Another related area was intellectual property. As well as copyright pertaining to the recorded speech, the researcher also had to consider the copyright in the photographs and narratives contributed by participants. They decided to ask participants for joint copyright and, in response to our advice, permission to use the photographs for any research activity without restriction.

We strongly encouraged them to use the institutional storage provision. They took up our suggestions of third party tools for editing the metadata of recordings and photographs, but decided against our suggestion of using an external transcription service, preferring to employ a research associate for the task. After discussing the services the University could offer for hosting the bricolage, we agreed it would be better to use an external solution, and directed them to Purchasing Services for advice on selecting a web development company.

We were fortunate to have been involved so early in the discussions, as the researcher had the right information to hand when she came to write her DMP for the ESRC. Thus when she sent the plan to us for review, it was already in good shape. Possibly our most important contribution at this point was to help the researcher achieve the right level of detail to get the important information across in three pages.

The researcher was grateful for our help, and has come back to us again for help with archiving data from another project and with a DMP for a third. We were pleased to learn that the first application was successful and at the time of writing is just starting up.

Experiences like this are tremendously rewarding. It is a great feeling to know that, not only have we helped the researcher build a stronger bid, but she will be going into the project well prepared for the challenges ahead, and will end the project with a high quality dataset to add to the scientific record. We have also found that providing this service has a snowball effect. The quality of plans coming from researchers we have helped before is noticeably higher; and when one person has a good experience, they seem to tell their colleagues, resulting in a flood of new enquiries!

The previous two stories show the importance of taking time to get steeped in the research in question before offering advice. As in the case of some of the earlier vignettes, good use was made of the tools of the data trade: DCPs, DAF, DMPonline and so on. Following this the support teams scheduled a face to face meeting with the researcher (or the whole research group) and asked questions until they understood the research project's aims sufficiently. In this way, the data professionals gained the confidence needed to give project-specific advice without haste. By working together as partners, the researcher and the data professional come to mutually recognize and affirm each other's respective areas of expertise.

The snowball effect of data management plans

As these vignettes have demonstrated, the provision of data management services can take a variety of forms depending on the needs of the researchers and institution, but there are common stages that can be covered. The creation of a DMP is one, and it can be used as a point of entry – a calling card – to introduce researchers to the support that is available to them. A consistent theme in these descriptions is that successful support in this one key area can have a snowball effect. It not only attracts the attention of researchers but also draws them in to all the other concerns of RDM. Positive comment spreads quickly within departments and it is greatly appreciated when researchers, struggling to complete DMPs, are able to receive advice that addresses a direct concern. Early involvement in the research lifecycle, if maintained, also allows a fuller relationship to develop over time when advice can be given on other key stages. Those working to deliver research support also benefit as they improve their data management competencies (Davis and Cross, 2015), gain a fuller understanding of the work in progress at their institution and develop new discipline insights.

Like a snowball this work can also be a time sensitive event. As researchers become more experienced in completing DMPs they may no longer need as much support in completing them. Successful plans will be shared – either through a deliberate strategy of the data management infrastructure or at an informal departmental level – and this will accelerate the process of independence.

When read together these vignettes demonstrate that RDM is not only concerned with funding applications or archiving datasets. These practical examples show the wide range of issues that can be discussed between a researcher and a data professional and that the value of DMPs go beyond simply fulfilling a requirement of a funding application. If maintained as living documents they can also record the evolution a research project undergoes after funding has been awarded. For the data librarian or data professional they provide an opportunity to engage with research projects, increase their knowledge and contribute to developing a stronger culture of good research practice, preservation and re-use.

Key take-away points

- A DMP is required by most funding bodies and offers a good opportunity for data librarians to get involved with projects at an early stage.
- A DMP should be prepared as early as possible and may be used as a way of promoting a wider range of data management services.
- Tools for creating DMPs include DMPonline, DMPtool as well as advice pages and checklists from the California Digital Library, the ICPSR, UKDA and similar organizations.
- The whole of the research lifecycle is covered by a DMP including methodological issues, information security, governance, ethics, funder requirements and issues of digital technology.
- Research into DMP requirements for specific funders can be a good way of increasing your expertise and confidence in the fact that you are developing a service that is in demand.
- DMPs in themselves are not complicated – but they are unfamiliar to many researchers who sometimes simply need reassurance or feedback rather than detailed advice.
- Success in offering assistance with DMPs often results in stronger funding applications and attracts the attention of researchers.
- DMPs can go beyond meeting funder requirements if regularly revised and can be used as an essential tool for managing a research project.

Reflective questions

1. What support should you offer in explaining, preparing or evaluating DMPs?
2. To what extent can you liaise with pre-existing support departments in your organization rather than duplicating effort?
3. How can your own experience of assisting with DMPs be used to develop the future direction of support services?
4. Should standardized text be offered for key sections of a DMP or should each be considered a bespoke document?
5. Should you plan to have long-term and repeated involvement with research projects or is it more likely that researchers will quickly absorb your advice and become confident in these issues? What are the advantages and disadvantages of each?

CHAPTER 7
Essentials of data repositories

Repository versus archive?

What is a data repository and what is a data archive? We do not have any definitive answers and opinions often vary, but it is useful to note how the terms are used in practice. Certainly in one sense the two terms are synonymous. Each term carries with it certain implied characteristics, and is used within its own contexts and traditions. Social science data archives, as we discussed in Chapter 1, have a tradition going back decades. They can be established at various levels, most commonly national or sub-institutional, such as departmental. The term 'archive' to some implies rigorous long-term preservation procedures, and can also be associated with long-term storage that is not publicly accessible. In some cases these are collections intended to become open at some point in the future for legal reasons, also known as 'dark archives'. To others, 'archive' is seen as a simple IT storage service akin to long-term back-up, but without any of the added curation that helps keep data usable and understandable over time and across communities ('keeping the bits safe'). Of course the word archive is both a noun and a verb and the demand to 'archive research data' is a common one; but we suggest that on closer examination there is not enough shared understanding among communities about what it means to 'archive your data'. For this reason we feel the term is best avoided, except as part of a name of a known institution.

Data repositories have a different provenance. Digital repositories came into fashion in the early 2000s to manage and disseminate publications and other types of digital assets. The use of 'repository' rather than 'archive' may in part indicate a desire to differentiate them from traditional physical archives managed within institutions. Electronic or digital repositories such as these were usually based on open source software such as DSpace, EPrints, Fedora and others, and were broadly established in institutions, championed by academic libraries in support of the open access movement. In addition to publications repositories, other specialist collections such as e-learning repositories began to flourish as well. Some repositories are subject-based, such as the well known arXiv service, established in 1991 for disseminating e-prints (electronic preprints) of scientific papers in the fields of mathematics, physics, astronomy, computer science and related fields.

Data repositories are sometimes domain-specific and may be associated with large data centres, such as the NERC-sponsored British Atmospheric Data Centre. Increasingly, institutional repositories are accepting research data as a content type, or librarians are building new institutional data repositories alongside their publications repositories or campus or current research information systems (CRIS), and creating linkages between them. Repositories seem to emphasize access over preservation, yet many of the first institutional repositories had the word 'archive' in their name. A widespread use of the term 'trusted digital repository' also shows the desire to bring archiving and preservation back into the frame. It remains to be seen how many institutional repositories will prioritize the achievement of trusted digital repository status, through self-audit, peer assessment or ISO 16363 certification.

A number of efforts at registering existing data repositories globally have come together in the form of the Registry of Research Data Repositories website (www.re3data.org), now an imprint of DataCite. Over 1500 repositories have been registered and can be found through a search engine or application programming interface (API). Whether all of these should be trusted or recommended to users is another issue.

Put, get, search: what is a repository?

Before discussing data repositories in particular, it may be useful to continue pursuing a definition of a digital repository. A widely cited definition is from Clifford Lynch, who characterized 'a university-based institutional repository [as] a set of services that a university offers to the members of its community for the management and dissemination of digital materials created by the institution and its community members' (Lynch, 2003, 2). In their 2005 review of all types of digital repositories within academia, Heery and Anderson differentiated digital repositories from other forms of digital collections, such as digital libraries, databases, catalogues and directories, by asserting that repositories have these essential characteristics:

- content is deposited in a repository, whether by the content creator, owner or a third party
- the repository architecture manages content as well as metadata
- the repository offers a minimum set of basic services e.g. put, get, search, access control

- the repository must be sustainable and trusted, well-supported and well-managed.

(Heery and Anderson, 2005, 1–2)

Repository platforms
Repositories can be built from scratch for a particular purpose, such as Figshare from Digital Science, but more often they are based on an existing software platform. These can be either open source or proprietary. As noted above, leading examples of common open source platforms are DSpace, Fedora and EPrints. DSpace and Fedora are now maintained by a not-for-profit organization in the USA called Duraspace, and both happen to be built in the same programming language, Java. DSpace is marketed as a turnkey solution, which works 'out of the box' without the need for extensive customization. It was originally created by MIT Libraries and Hewlett Packard to manage all types of digital objects produced by a university. It is the most common repository system used worldwide. An example of a data repository based on DSpace is Dryad. Fedora is a more sophisticated system, which requires additional software for its user interface. It is particularly appealing because of its flexible data model and seems to be popular with those for whom robust digital preservation is paramount. Both Hydra and Islandora are based on Fedora but offer more features (such as a user interface). EPrints was created at Southampton University in the UK in the Perl language, and is maintained by developers there. The developers and maintainers of EPrints are responsive to the needs of UK institutional repositories, making it the top choice among UK institutions for institutional repositories. Other free and open source options often chosen explicitly for RDM are The Dataverse, developed at Harvard University, Invenio, developed at CERN (used by the Zenodo repository), and the Comprehensive Kerbal Archive Network (CKAN), developed by the Open Knowledge Foundation (used by several government open data portals).

Hosted solutions are available for purchase by institutions without software developers or administrators who can support systems. A proprietary solution sometimes used by institutions is a CRIS, which is designed to manage an institution's body of research activity comprehensively, from grant proposals to research outputs. Examples are Pure from Elsevier, Converis from Thomson Reuters, and Symplectic Elements. One of the attractions of such systems is the ability to showcase people, projects and research outputs systematically. One open source product that does this is VIVO, a semantic web application developed at Cornell now run by Duraspace. Sometimes these systems are implemented so as to interoperate with an institutional repository and sometimes they take the place of the repository entirely. This model is being followed at the University of Oxford where ORA-Data is being developed in-house but also makes use of Symplectic for certain functions. Cloud services are also making their way into the repository space, with many UK institutions adopting Arkivum for long-term storage of research data, Figshare for Institutions, or Duracloud from Duraspace. The field is bound to get more crowded with options, and this will give data librarians a role in spelling out exactly what is on offer to their researchers. They will also need to show how the repository they are involved with is distinctive and works alongside existing alternative options for data deposit.

Scoping your data repository

In some sense, debating pros and cons of repository software can be left to the techies. But once technical questions about these systems are resolved, they need to be developed, managed and promoted so as to engage with the rest of the institution. Academic libraries are in a good position to set up and run institutional and/or data repositories, because in addition to being 'close to the researchers' who produce the data, they are long-lived institutions set up to preserve and disseminate the scholarly record, of which data increasingly are seen to be an essential part.

How the data repository – or institutional repository which will now accept data – interacts with related institutional systems is a key question. Will the library rely on IT services to administer and run the platform of the repository? Is there sufficient separation between the hardware and software infrastructure on which the researchers need to work with their data while it is 'live' (whether local, central or cloud-based) and the repository, which will provide access to completed research outputs? For example, Edinburgh University has decided to differentiate not only its active data storage (DataStore) from its data repository (DataShare), but it has also kept DataShare purely as a public access data repository (with time-limited embargoes permitted), and developed a separate DataVault (long-term storage) service for individual research projects in which the data cannot be publicly shared. Such restricted data can include research records, personal and sensitive forms of data, key versions of data or other 'golden copies', data which the researcher does not have the rights to share, and under-documented datasets. Explaining the difference between services has been challenging (there is also a related service, DataSync, which has Dropbox-like features for collaborating with others), and so they have been combined into an overarching 'research data service' to compensate for the complexity of choices (www.ed.ac.uk/is/research-data-service).

Guidance also needs to be clear regarding when it is appropriate for researchers to deposit in a disciplinary repository instead of an institutional repository, or even a specialized departmental repository within the institution. Some researchers may have a long history of depositing their research data and be unwilling to switch to a newer institutional repository. Others may have no alternatives and demand to use such a repository, or prefer to out of institutional pride. The University of Oxford Bodleian Library gives the following advice: 'Some disciplines are well served by established and well known data archives. Examples include the UKDA, Dryad, GenBank, [European Molecular Biology Laboratory] and the NERC [data centres]. Deposit in some of these archives is dependent on funding body or publisher. . . . However the fact remains that some disciplines do not have obvious locations for archiving data' (http://researchdata.ox.ac.uk/preserving-your-data/archives-and-other-options). The same source offers a tabular representation of options to consider in preserving, sharing and citing data, in which features of ORA-Data are compared against other services. Data librarians may feel free to encourage depositing data locally where there is no clear preference on the part of the researcher or their funder. Seeding the repository with datasets from a number of departments is important, as it helps to build trust within the institution's research community towards the repository.

The authors' two institutions participated in the Jisc-funded DISC-UK (Data Information Specialists Committee-UK) project from March 2007 to July 2009, which led to a number of deliverables including *Policy-making for Research Data in Repositories* (Green, Macdonald and Rice, 2009). The guide may be used as a decision-making and planning tool for institutions with digital repositories in existence or in development, that are considering adding research data to their digital collections. It was deemed crucial that the data repository should include in its scope or coverage:

- subjects and languages
- kinds of research data (e.g. observational, experimental, computational)
- status of the research data (for example, preliminary data, only those which underlie published research results, or only fully documented datasets)
- versions
- data file formats
- volume and size limitations.

Decisions about what nature of data to accept in the repository, based on such criteria as the above, need to be made in advance to avoid 'mission-creep' – a common phenomenon of institutional repositories set up for one purpose, which then lose focus as they attempt to meet shifting demands.

If the repository is capturing multidisciplinary data produced across the university, then the repository administrators need to decide who has the right to deposit (research staff, students, collaborators, ex-staff, alumni) and a method of authentication and authorization needs to be adopted to manage logins; preferably the same 'single sign-on' login that they use for other university services.

Choosing a metadata schema

Metadata alone may not be a reason to manage data in a separate repository from other research outputs, unless your service can benefit from a structural (such as XML-based) metadata standard that applies to homogeneous datasets – data of similar type or structure. For example, if all of your data are survey or other similarly structured microdata files, you may gain the full benefit of the DDI metadata standard, which allows you to mark up data right down to the variable level. This facilitates use of a dedicated system to browse, subset and even perform online analysis with the data. The Dataverse.org platform developed at Harvard University and available as a cloud service and open source software is one solution that allows such an approach; other comparable solutions include Nesstar and Survey Documentation and Analysis. However, if your collection includes primarily other data formats from across the spectrum of research in which your institution engages, this may not be feasible, and a download-only model may be the best you can achieve, in which case a more generic type of repository system may be perfectly suitable.

It will be comforting for many used to the traditional world of library administration to learn that many of the bibliographic metadata fields applied to publications can apply to datasets, at least for purposes of discovery. Once depositors get over the shock of having to give their dataset a name – which need not be the same as the accompanying research article – they generally adapt to filling in other fields such as 'data creator(s)', 'data publisher' and the all-important 'data description'. For the most part, this takes care of two important functions:

- allowing search engines to index landing pages to datasets and make the dataset discoverable through everyday searches and specialized facilities such as Google Scholar
- allowing citations to be built from basic metadata fields, which is one of the keys to enabling data creators to receive credit for producing and sharing data.

Then datasets can share a schema with publications because at the most general level metadata for datasets are like metadata for publications. It also makes it possible to apply metadata schemas created for bibliographic or other material to datasets, such as the well known Dublin Core, or its more complex offspring, 'DCterms', maintained by the Dublin Core Metadata Initiative.

Converging on a standard: DataCite metadata and digital object identifiers
In addition to discipline-specific metadata standards, a general metadata standard for datasets has emerged in recent years. DataCite, which is both a metadata standard (e.g. DataCite 4.0) and an international organization set up to promote the standard and mint DOIs for datasets, dictates six mandatory fields:

- identifier
- creator
- title
- publisher
- publication year
- resource type.

Clearly, these are the fields needed to create an adequate citation. DOIs for datasets can only be obtained through a DataCite provider. In most situations, an organization will decide to subscribe to a DataCite member organization (such as the British Library in the UK) which requires paying a flat annual fee for minting any number of DOIs with one's own institutional 'prefix'.

It should be pointed out that DOIs are not the only type of persistent identifiers; in fact DOIs are based on the handle system (handle.net), and are available for a very inexpensive registration fee. The main advantage of using DOIs over other systems is that because Crossref DOIs are commonly used in the publishing world, it helps to make datasets respected as something that can (and indeed should) be cited along with a publication in a reference list or bibliography. In addition, some authors may believe that possessing a DOI gives their digital object a higher status than other objects on the internet, adding another incentive to deposit their data in your repository. The advantage of any type of persistent identifier is that they remain valid longer than a given URL, because they can be remapped when content moves between websites or onto some unknown network in the future. Of course this depends on either the organizations (DataCite, Handle.net, etc.) surviving, or somebody taking over the job of resolving the identifiers on their sites.

No matter what system is used, the institution minting the identifiers (such as your own) needs to take responsibility for ensuring that each of the identifiers resolve to an authentic location. Normally it will be a landing page providing metadata and links to data files. This means that persistent identifiers should only be minted for content that your organization intends to keep and manage for the long term. If the material is to be maintained by others, and your organization is merely pointing to it, minting a persistent identifier is ill-advised.

Another practical tip relates to non-persistence – when an item has to be removed from a collection. When content must be withdrawn for whatever reason – which may include legal challenges, retractions, corrected versions or future collections reappraisal, a 'tombstone record' should be maintained with the original metadata, noting that the item has been withdrawn on a given date. This is good practice in any case, whether DOIs or other identifiers, or even just URLs, are used.

Additional fields certainly add value to the metadata record and enhance the usability of the data. Each repository needs to balance the number of fields provided with the willingness of depositors or available staff resources to enter additional metadata. If assisted deposit is offered, the depositor will know even less about the dataset than the data creator, and may be unable to complete many fields. A compromise is to mandate a minimum number of fields, and simply encourage depositors to fill in additional ones where applicable. User testing can be invaluable for discovering the tolerance levels of depositors (at what point do they simply give up trying?), the most appropriate context-sensitive help or hint text, and those questions that cause frustration due to lack of understanding or lack of applicability to the data creator's field.

The past and present metadata schemas of Edinburgh DataShare are available on a wiki (www.wiki.ed.ac.uk/display/datashare/DataShare). DataCite 4.0 is expected to be adopted. DataCite's 4.0 schema includes the following additional (recommended and optional) metadata fields (http://doi.org/10.5438/0012):

- subject
- contributor
- date
- language
- alternate identifier
- related identifier
- size
- format
- version
- rights
- description
- geo location
- funding reference.

Managing access

Arguably, there are four kinds of access conditions associated with any data repository or archive:

1. Open access – anyone with access to the public internet may access the data; the data may have terms of use specified, or indicate appropriate or inappropriate use through a standard licence (such as the Creative Commons suite). Normally anonymous access to data are provided but in some cases a name and e-mail address may be requested before access is granted.
2. Managed access – rules may apply to the use of the data, for example users may not only need to register but also be approved before access is granted. Approval may depend on the status of the user (e.g. member of an academic institution), or their answers to questions, for example about their research question, or the objective of the research.
3. Secure access – data are only released through certain secure mechanisms. These may involve accessing a remote server to run analyses rather than downloading data directly; having output checked by repository staff to ensure non-disclosure of personal or sensitive information; undertaking a training course or having one's analysis procedures vetted in detail before access is granted; travelling to a specified location to access data on a non-networked computer; or agreeing to a legally binding contract in which data handling and management tools, rules or standards are specified and signed by the researcher and an institutional contact.
4. Closed access – a metadata record is publicly available but the data are not readily accessible to users. There may be a time-limited embargo blocking access, or the item may have been withdrawn for some reason.

Clearly the four kinds of access are associated with increasing levels of effort on the part of repository staff. Only the first involves potentially no mediation by staff, though effort may be required at the point of deposit – or 'ingest' in Open Archival Information System (OAIS) terminology, see the section 'Trusted digital repositories' below – to ensure that terms of use or licences are attached as appropriate. Depositors and data creators must also understand the terms under which the data are being disseminated. This may involve explaining open licences generally, or what specific 'flavours' of licence do, or emphasizing to depositors and data creators that once data have been accessed from the repository, use of the data or violation of the terms is unlikely to be policed; the data are, in effect, 'in the wild'.

The reason this point matters is that most people, and many academics, are not aware of the difference between open access 'gratis' and open access 'libre'. The first means anyone may have a copy of the item for free, but any copyright restrictions or licence terms remain in place; the second means in addition to simply having a copy of the data for one's own use, explicit permission to make copies and disseminate the data is given (normally through an open licence). Non-commercial licences (where re-use is permitted except for commercial purposes) are not considered true open licences by many open data advocates and should be used with caution, albeit they are intuitively attractive to many. Further context about open access and open data licences is given in Chapter 10.

Data quality review (or be kind to your end-users)

Key policy decisions for repository managers regard the extent of quality control to be applied at the deposit stage. Similar decisions will also be needed about the amount of ongoing curation to be applied, and the level of commitment to digital preservation over the long term. This depends on the vision and mission of the repository, taking into account stakeholder expectations, staffing resources (full-time equivalents and expertise) and of course funding.

Assumptions about the value of the data that are being deposited are an important issue. If the data are seen as a lesser-value addition to open access research publications in a combined institutional repository, then special techniques and procedures are unlikely to be developed and applied. However, unlike a repository of 'green' open access publications, the research data deposited in a repository are likely to be the only copies available, other than perhaps a few images, tables or graphs that appear in a published article, making the data unique additions to the scholarly record. The curation of research data during ingest may also be regarded as an opportunity to add great value to deposits in terms of documentation and contextualization. Debate is ongoing about the efficacy of 'self-archiving' and the strengths and limitations associated with it. This, combined with the lack of practice most researchers have in preparing data for deposit, is reason to consider applying more extensive quality control and curation effort at the ingest stage. If only to recognize the old computing adage, GIGO: Garbage In, Garbage Out, one should have some minimal set of rules about data deposit.

A rule for Edinburgh DataShare, for example, is that at least one (human-readable) documentation file must be included. This may be simply be a readme.txt file explaining what the various files are in a dataset and how they relate to each other, or it may be the full list of variable or column labels in a dataset (data dictionary). The point is to prevent burdening the end-user of the dataset with needing to decipher a list of cryptic abbreviations. Other types of documentation may be a technical or methodology report, questionnaire, codebook, manual or other explanatory material, possibly including the research article that explained the results of the data (if IPR allows).

The University of Bristol's Research Data Repository requires a readme.txt file with each deposit:

> Your readme file must include:
>
> - An inventory of the major parts of the dataset, so users can identify any missing parts
> - Details of any particular operating system required to make use of the data
> - Details of any particular software required to make use of the data
> - Information about any other dependencies (e.g. particular libraries) required to make use of the data
> - For tabular data, descriptions of column headings and row labels, any data codes used and units of measurements.
>
> (http://goo.gl/ZHGWT2)

Similarly, rules may require certain metadata fields when documenting deposits. As mentioned in the metadata section above, the minimum metadata for a public repository should allow the user to create a suitable citation of the dataset and understand the terms of re-use, whereas other fields may enhance discoverability. Disciplinary repositories can afford to be more specific about minimal structural metadata that enhance re-use. Experimental biology fields have adopted standards of 'minimum information' required for reproducibility, such as Minimum Information About a Microarray Experiment (MIAME; http://fged.org/projects/miame).

Any quality control that can be applied at the point of deposit (and before), will save time, effort and frustration if the data are later deemed worthy of curation, or if a user requests assistance in using the data. Since it is difficult to assess the value of a given dataset or the interest that it may garner over time, it is worth systematizing quality control checks for every dataset deposited, e.g. through checklists. Edinburgh DataShare has both a depositor-facing 'Checklist for Deposit' (http://edin.ac/1cqvxQc) and a checklist for repository administrators on a wiki, 'Checking a New Item Submission to DataShare' (http://edin.ac/1EYhiOT). Table 7.1 gives the flavour of the content of each.

Getting the balance right between haranguing a potential depositor for missing documentation and metadata versus taking advantage of the only moment you may have that researcher's attention before an item is accepted into the repository is a diplomatic art, which improves with practice. It helps to think of oneself as an advocate for the silent, future data user. The

Table 7.1 *Checklists for depositors and repository administrators*
Source: Edinburgh DataShare (http://edin.ac/1cqvxQc and http://edin.ac/1EYhiOT).

Checklist for depositors	Checklist for repository administrators
Step 1 – Set up your profile	Check whether the Submission has been added to an existing Collection
Step 2 – Group your files into datasets (items)	Check that all the files can be opened/read
Step 3 – Prepare your data	Check the size of the files. Check the filetypes against the DataShare File Registry
Step 4 – Prepare your documentation	Check that metadata are reasonably complete and contain no typos. Check that there is appropriate documentation
Step 5 – Permissions and rights	Check the rights statement
Step 6 – Decide if an embargo is needed	
Step 7 – Consider an open licence	

approach to quality review can then improve the actual usefulness of the material being preserved as well as reinforce the commitment of an institution to developing and sustaining a repository. To get a sense of what a high level of quality control in a data repository service looks like, we recommend reading the article 'Committing to Data Quality Review' (Peer, Green and Stephenson, 2014).

Digital preservation planning across space and time

A number of factors contribute to what is called the fragility of digital material. These range from hardware and software issues to cultural change over time. Digital preservation is usually thought of as a requirement to prevent decay of material over time, or to maintain continuity of access for future users. But some of the remedies are equally useful for addressing accessibility issues in the present: to make material useful across space, to members of distant communities, audiences – such as those who use another language or are simply in another discipline – who do not have access to the same computing environments or have the same shared tacit knowledge that allow members within communities to share data easily and informally among themselves. Making data accessible across space and time requires explicit planning. For this reason, researchers are advised to pass on their completed research outputs to digital 'stewards' such as data librarians and data archivists who make it their business to maintain continuity of access. By depositing data in a trusted repository, researchers can ensure that they and other data users will have continued access to their data, in ways they cannot through informal sharing or merely posting data on a website.

Digital preservation is a research field in itself as well as a community of practice. There are many difficult unsolved problems and changes in tactics over time. We would advise repository managers to become involved with at least one group that concerns itself with digital preservation in order to keep up with emerging standards of practice, to begin to absorb terminology and adapt it to one's own context. This is a highly interpretive domain, particularly because all digital preservation actions cost money (resources, time and effort), and nobody quite knows which actions will pay off in the future. David Rosenthal's blog (http://blog.dshr.org) is worth monitoring for thoughtful and provocative economic arguments about digital preservation planning. A look at some key digital preservation concepts and their generally accepted remedies follows, with tips about how to plan a service to take them into account.

'Bit rot' is the decay over time of individual bits that make up files, especially ones that do not get processed and therefore copied very often. Depending on which bits actually rot, this may make the file unreadable (technically speaking we mean un-renderable), or it may make information disappear in an unnoticed part of the file. Computed 'checksums' are one remedy: these are machine-readable records (or a string of characters) that provide a fingerprint of a digital file and can normally detect bit rot by comparing the old and new checksum of a file. To use these in a repository environment, one must plan to capture a checksum on ingest, and to check them at regular intervals, or use a system that does so automatically and reports discrepancies. Of course in some cases the media themselves are what decays and becomes unreadable. A remedy for this problem is to store media appropriately – especially offline storage such as back-up tapes, or CDs and DVDs – and refresh those media on a schedule designed to avoid decay. For this reason online storage (e.g. disc space on servers) may be preferable, even for files not accessed very often, but is generally more expensive. No storage solution completely solves the bit rot problem over time; rather the problem needs to be managed.

'Format obsolescence' is another oft-cited problem of digital preservation. Currently many libraries are needing to retire CD-ROMs not due to any physical deterioration but because the format is no longer compatible with newer operating systems and hardware. A number of further prominent examples exist from prior decades: even software so commonplace as Microsoft Word and SPSS failed at times to ensure 'backward compatibility' of software: the ability to read their own previous versions of files in current software programs. Companies seem to be more alert to this problem now, as they suffer reputational damage, but suppliers may still go out of business, be bought out, or not maintain the format. However help is at hand as there are at least three remedies backed by digital preservation experts: format migration, emulation and prescription.

'Format migration' is the commitment to actively migrate formats to new software versions before they are at risk of becoming obsolete (which may not happen for several versions). This may or may not make sense for a repository service to commit to doing for a specified number of format types. It can be time consuming and dependent on human labour. On the other hand, if there are that many files in the repository to make it time consuming then it may be considered foolish not to do it. A policy or depositor agreement may be necessary to obtain the rights to make such changes to deposited files, because aspects of the information may change (such as look and feel, or loss of customized content such as spreadsheet formulae).

The second remedy is 'emulation': this is the engineering of new software that can read an obsolete format and render it in the same way that the original software did. Unsurprisingly, gaming enthusiasts have pioneered much of the work in this area. This strategy would not normally be chosen by repository managers aiming to maintain access over time: but it may provide a pay-off for an identified body of otherwise lost material. Java virtual machines are a kind of preventative version of emulation: repositories may wish to accept versions of software code saved this way in the hope that they will be able to run on any computing platform in the future.

The third strategy is 'prescription': only to accept file formats that conform to standard preservation formats; a variation is only to accept files that have open formats. Standard preservation formats are broadly known and understood, either through a specification agreed by a standards organization such as the ISO (International Standards Organization) or because of wide-term use. PDF tends to be thought of as a de facto standard, although it is owned by Adobe, which provides open documentation of the proprietary format. (Technically there are numerous PDF formats all with the .pdf suffix, some of which may be more broadly readable than others.) The difficulty with prescription is that research is both diverse and fast-changing and it is hard for a repository manager to be knowledgeable about all possible formats. The adage that 'the great thing about standards is that there are so many to choose from' holds, and in our experience researchers will choose many of them and for varied reasons, so much so that we often learn about new formats from our users. At the same time there is great value in prescription when researchers are looking for advice about what formats they should be using.

Trusted digital repositories

Pursuing trusted digital repository status can help your repository gain credibility and help you achieve your digital preservation planning objectives. The Data Seal of Approval (DSA) was developed by a social science data archive in the Netherlands – DANS – in 2008, and since 2009 has been managed by an international board of experts elected by the DSA General Assembly. The criteria for assigning a DSA to data repositories comply with national and international guidelines for digital data archiving.

An interesting feature of the DSA is that it accords responsibility to three actors: the data producer, the data consumer (user) and of course the data repository. This presumes that the data producer must take some responsibility for future-proofing their data, as well as making it understandable to researchers who might not be working in the same field, or have access to the same resources or software. Similarly, the data user must take some responsibility for ensuring the data are of sufficient quality to be useful in their own research (*caveat emptor*). The repository manages and curates the data and interacts with data producers and data consumers to help them make the best use of the data.

The DSA is one type of 'trust standard', and is generally considered the one with the lowest bar to entry. Others include audit and certification of trustworthy digital repositories (ISO 16363) and Criteria for Trustworthy Digital Archives (DIN 31644). All of them build on the more established standard of the OAIS Reference Model developed by the space science community, and use much of its terminology. OAIS was developed out of the necessity of preserving digital data collected from space beginning in the previous century (even NASA made some mistakes) and became an ISO standard in 2003; it was updated in 2012 (ISO 14721:2012) with input from the archival community (Consultative Committee for Space Data Systems, 2012).

The need for interoperability

An institutional data repository may well be part of another system – such as a closed or private storage system with an open access 'toggle' – or a new feature in the institution's publications repository. In any case it is important that the data repository be as interoperable as possible. The last thing the world needs is another data silo, which adds value and gives context to the data within, but is disconnected from the internet or inaccessible.

For example, often there is a primary publication (or more than one publication) that is closely associated with the dataset. Metadata records need to include links to these, and preferably publications will also link back to datasets. In some cases depositors will want DOIs or URLs for the data to include in a publication submitted for review. If the data are not to be released before publication, this can be accomplished through the use of an embargo period.

In what other ways should a data repository aim to be interoperable? One common method used in online systems is an API, which allows a system to get information and pass information to other systems through a set of programming instructions and protocols. An API may be supplied only to trusted partners or it may be made publicly available. Although the use of APIs is currently widespread, it is actually not a standards-based way of exchanging information (because each system uses its own set of instructions to which the second system needs to conform). Many APIs do use representational state transfer (REST), which simplifies operations such as 'put' and 'get' by using the http protocol of the world wide web. A RESTful API is desirable for its simplicity, which reduces likelihood of performance overload, etc.

Standards-based ways of achieving equivalent passing of information can include the Open Archives Initiative Protocol for Metadata Harvesting (OAI-PMH) and linked open data. OAI-PMH is a repository-specific standard that builds on Dublin Core to allow harvesting of records, for example to an aggregator service or portal. Linked open data, also known as the semantic web, is a way of semantically linking and querying sources of information, which relies on data to be marked up in RDF using openly defined metadata vocabularies.

Other important ways for data repositories to be inter-connected are to use services described in earlier chapters. They could be registered in a data repository registry such as Re3Data.org, so that people will be able to discover the repository, and to consider using a persistent identifier (PID) service such as DataCite, so that the repository may be found through a lookup of its items' PIDs. Thomson Reuters' Data Citation Index also harvests content from selected data repositories in order to track citations of datasets in the literature. Use of international name authority systems such as ORCID (Open Researcher and Contributor ID) will help link data creators with other outputs they produce and their collaborators.

As well as being interoperable, a trusted repository should be FAIR. The Data FAIRport initiative (the name Fairport Convention having been taken!) began at a workshop in Leiden, the Netherlands, in 2014, and aims to make valuable scientific data Findable, Accessible, Interoperable and Re-usable (FAIR). How well do your datasets get surfaced in a Google (or other search engine) search? How clear is it to would-be users how they may obtain the data? There are a number of ways for repositories to ensure their data are re-usable, first and foremost of which is to ensure there is adequate metadata and other documentation, but also the ability to trace provenance and data versions, such as through timestamps and linking records.

One task for a data librarian is to try and assess what is needed and what is possible within their institutional setting. This chapter has outlined many of the features and decisions that are required. Emerging commercial services are also selling archival solutions; however, these solutions may fall short of what stakeholders want from repositories, or offer prohibitively expensive solutions for which funding can be difficult to obtain for anything other than minimum compliance. An ideal, fully formed service may be an aspiration but in practice we have to decide what is achievable at any given time. An understanding of the essentials is necessary in assessing the options open to you and what you can realistically undertake to deliver.

Key take-away points
- The word archive means different things to different people. Explain your terms to users.
- Over 1500 data repositories are registered on re3data.org.
- There are a number of open source platforms to choose from in building a repository.
- Creating policies, particularly regarding scope, is an important step in setting up a repository.
- For purposes of discovery, metadata for datasets look similar to metadata for publications.
- There are arguably four kinds of access conditions for datasets: open, managed, secure and closed (including embargoed).
- A good opportunity to add value to a dataset is at the point of deposit.
- Digital preservation concepts such as bit rot, format obsolescence, emulation, format prescription and migration need to be considered for decision-making about data curation.
- Working towards a trusted digital repository standard can lend credibility to your repository and help you with decisions about digital preservation.
- Interoperability is another important goal for your digital repository service.

Reflective questions
1. What is the most important function of a repository to you: put, get, or search? Why?
2. Is it better to steer a researcher towards an institutional or a discipline-specific repository?
3. What are the advantages and disadvantages of hosting your repository locally versus using a hosting service or commercial solution?
4. What types of policies would you need in place to provide an open access data repository?
5. Which do you consider more important for a repository: digital preservation or interoperability?

CHAPTER 8
Dealing with sensitive data

Challenging assumptions about data

What is meant by confidential or sensitive data? In Chapter 2 we outlined some of the formats of common types of research data. The field is of course wide and may include datasets that are based on numbers, text or audiovisual material. Most of the time researchers will be interested in how they can manipulate these in order to address the goals of their investigations. Some researchers are interested less in the format than in what they consider to be fundamental problems of confidentiality or data sensitivity. They have concerns about managing the data securely while they are working with it – and are unsure what they are supposed to do. Others have concerns about the appropriateness of allowing preservation or re-use of the same material. Understanding what a researcher actually means when they state their data are confidential therefore becomes significant. This is a growing area of discussion and is demonstrated by the huge interest shown by researchers in training and awareness raising courses on this topic. Typical concerns include whether the data:

1 were collected just for a specific research project
2 are still needed for future analysis
3 may only be properly understood by the original researchers
4 should be destroyed once they have been used or analysed
5 could be exploited for non-academic purposes
6 cover a subject area that is not for public consumption such as studies of terrorists, family history or locations of endangered species
7 contain general information that could allow participants to be identified
8 include names and addresses or similar personal information
9 include particular details that could be harmful to participants if made public

10 are to be treated as confidential so an unintended release *in itself* would be damaging.

Such a wide range of concerns illustrates that no data type is inherently more confidential than another. It is possible to encounter variations on some or all of these arguments from researchers working with statistical data, video interviews or samples of genetic material. However it is commonplace to find researchers working under the assumption that all their data are confidential and present unique problems. The role of the data librarian is to help shift that perception. Naturally there will be many occasions in which some confidential and sensitive data are actually created and manipulated for analysis. However that is not the same as acknowledging that all datasets need to be viewed in this way. The shift in perception needed is to see such material as an exception to most of the material being created rather than as an immediate block to any participation in preserving and sharing.

The tendency is to assume everything is made problematic by the presence of confidential or sensitive data and that the simplest solution is to withhold or destroy the data. It does not matter whether it is a small or large proportion of the content. The drive towards preserving, sharing and re-using research data being encouraged by funders, institutions and other stakeholders makes such 'head in the sand' views even more untenable. The challenge for those working in research support is to offer mechanisms and channels of information that help assess and evaluate the appropriateness of such concerns. After communicating that working with confidential or sensitive data does not ipso facto exempt academics from engaging with RDM and sharing, it is necessary to start addressing some of their actual concerns.

Understanding how researchers view their research

The research lifecycle is a popular way of describing the process of conducting academic research. Unfortunately it is not an especially exciting phrase and it singularly fails to convey the emotional attachment many academics have with their work. The data they are producing represent a great deal of time and effort so it is not surprising they may form a strong emotional bond to them. This is the first thing a data librarian needs to appreciate when assessing concerns around potentially sensitive data. Psychologically some researchers may not be ready to consider what happens to datasets after they have finished with them. Their concerns about allowing preservation or re-use of data are grounded in the loss of exclusive access to their data or a reluctance to pass it on for others to re-use. Reminders about funding obligations or publishers' expectations may be useful at these points. More importantly data librarians need to understand that such issues may not always be based on the content of the data but rather on the researchers' general attitudes regarding re-use.

Concerns about the usefulness or appropriateness of making datasets available to others (addressed above by typical concerns 1–4 in the list about the sensitivity of data) may need discussion and negotiation. It may be that a delay in depositing data or a time-limited embargo can be arranged to remove such concerns. Advice on supplying contextualizing documentation or a re-appraisal of undertakings regarding data destruction may also be useful. However in beginning to disentangle the knot of concerns a researcher may have, it is important to communicate to them that *these* are not inherently issues of confidentiality. While they may define it as a confidentiality problem it does not relate to the content of the dataset itself but to how they perceive and – just as importantly – have chosen to manage the problem.

Whenever possible it is important that confidential and sensitive data be discussed in terms of specific instances rather than general concerns. This allows practical solutions to be developed and offered to researchers. Anxiety about the potential for non-academic use by others (typical concern 5) is common and can be more easily addressed once specific instances are given. If the data creator has in mind use of the information by journalists or non-academic researchers then the danger is more clearly identified as are possible solutions. Allowing access through a managed process of registration involving applications and a statement on how the data will be used could be one solution. This will give depositors a sense of a rigorous process and an involvement in the future use of the data (should they wish).

It will also be an opportunity for a researcher to define what they consider as inappropriate access. This is preferable to restricting or specifying appropriate use since expectations of this are often quite limited. An academic assumes other researchers will generally wish to use their data in the same way as they have and within the same discipline. In fact, as has been noted, 'Re-use must also be considered outside the strict context of research in the discipline where the data is generated. Many of the most interesting re-use cases come from cross-disciplinary research. Data re-use can also occur outside academic research; re-use in learning and teaching is one example which is still of primary importance to universities' (Ashley, 2012, 155). While creators of a dataset may see the value of preserving it for verification they often have the least vision about how it could be repurposed in other ways. If the concern is more to do with commercial use of data then additional advice about an embargo – as well as dialogue with other institutional services that deal with commercial use of academic outputs – might be the direction to take.

Sensitivity and confidentiality – a general or specific problem?

Where does a data librarian start in understanding concerns about confidentiality? It is often important to assess whether the nature of a dataset is such that it is sensitive because of *general* or *particular* content. In the case of general content, confidentiality means the subject matter and therefore content as a whole is sensitive. Confidential elements cannot be easily separated and to attempt to do so would degrade the data or badly distort it (alluded to by typical concerns 6–7 in the list in the section 'Challenging assumptions about data' above) so that fine grain detail or meaning is lost.

In biomedical and other fields sensitivity may be economic and commercial in nature. Research often produces data that can lead to patents or be used to form the basis of new technologies. Isis Innovation, the research and technology commercialization company established by the University of Oxford, identifies areas such as 'healthcare and disease prevention: measuring healthcare outcomes; genetic testing; organ transplantation; TB vaccination; pre-natal screening; insect-borne disease control. . . . in energy demand, climate change, environmental sustainability: capturing sunlight; lightweight electric motors; assessing environmental impact' (www.isis-innovation.com/wp-content/uploads/2014/07/Isis-Impacts-FINAL.pdf). So clearly data may sometimes 'be considered proprietary information, as research is often funded by pharmaceutical and biomedical businesses seeking possible commercial applications' (Collins, 2012, 159). The company specifically set up to lead and manage the University's technology transfer and consulting activities, is just one example of this approach and most UK institutions have such spin-off companies. Aside from this there is also a well established tactic of defining some research and its data as commercial-in-confidence research. An approach must be agreed in advance under a contract or agreement of some sort worked out by the institution's research office and legal advisers. The agreement needs to clarify what rights the individual researchers and the university have in data and what can be done with them.

On the other hand a dataset which is confidential because of particular content will contain sensitive sections which are discrete and easily identifiable. They can therefore be tagged in advance or even removed (typical concerns 8–9 in the list 'Challenging assumptions about data' on page 21). This approach is the basis of most anonymization techniques in which predefined content is removed or replaced. When working with statistical survey data, for example, variables such as name, address and other identifying information may be systematically collected and analysed but then is easily removed (normally replaced with random case IDs) when the data are deposited and shared more widely. So you should encourage researchers to stop worrying generally about the fact that their data are confidential and instead focus on the specific content that presents a problem.

The strength of measures to protect this content can then be tested against real world scenarios of possible breaches of confidentiality. For example a survey of political participation in the workplace creates a dataset of responses. Researchers promise that no one's employers will be able to identify participants. In the original collected dataset sensitive content is present so it is not suitable for preservation or re-use. As a result it is assumed the dataset must be destroyed after it has been analysed. However, once negotiations about preserving the information focus on specific examples of how confidentiality could be breached, more options arise. Researchers may concede that specific variables allow individuals to be identified rather than all of the content, so if these are removed responses will not be associated with individuals. The rest of the data can be preserved and re-used.

Focusing on the most likely data breaches

Keeping imagined breaches of confidentiality rooted in the real world and actual working practices is a good strategy. It is more instructive and productive than thinking about theoretical breaches of confidentiality. It permits practical solutions to specific concerns to be developed and avoids the paralysing effect of ever longer lists of 'what ifs'. Concentration on the practical use of data and preventing the most likely ways they could be misused encourages continued usage while preserving confidentiality. Naturally less likely breaches can be dealt with after an initial secure framework is organized but attempts to deal with every eventuality can be overwhelming and suggest that it would be better to embargo or restrict access to all the data. The suitability of such techniques will vary from dataset to dataset and this is discussed in more detail later in this book, but at this stage it is enough to note this is another issue data librarians are well placed to advise on.

The biggest concerns over confidential or sensitive data usually emerge where research has included human subjects (live participants). In most cases researchers base their data collection on a series of agreements and undertakings in which they explain to potential subjects why they are collecting data, how it will be used and give them a chance to opt out. These agreements capture the consent respondents have given for the use of their contributions to a project (hence the coverage of them in Chapter 6). As a result participant consent agreements are crucial documents in establishing when content should or should not be seen as confidential. Some researchers may view such agreements as documentation that is mainly needed to win over respondents or to please ethics committees and which can be put aside once a project begins. In fact they should be seen as key documents that manage not only how information is collected but also describe the practical ways in which it is to be organized and used.

Participant consent agreements may vary in length and complexity. Some may simply be an acknowledgement of participation and a waiver of any claims on the content. Other agreements may explain how the information being gathered will be used and offer respondents the opportunity to withdraw from the study at any point. These understandings are often intended to encourage participation and it is not unusual to find agreements to destroy data once they have been used by a research team. One can imagine scenarios in which this may still be a tactic of last resort but in most cases researchers should be encouraged to see this as a counter-productive step. In addition because consent agreements establish the framework in which data and analysis proceed they are increasingly seen as documentation that needs to be fully worked out in the early stages of a project. There is plentiful advice on this available from university ethics departments and more widely from organizations such as the UKDA and the UK National Centre for Research Methods. Examples from the latter include the 'real life methods' series of guides such as 'Informed Consent in Visual Research' (http://eprints.ncrm. ac.uk/543/1/2008-07-toolkit-visual-consent.pdf) and 'Using Phone Interviews' (http://eprints.ncrm.ac.uk/1576/1/14-toolkit-phone-interviews.pdf).

A role in giving advice on consent agreements

For the data librarian the creation of consent agreements presents an excellent opportunity to get involved and provide feedback. Examples of consent agreements can be collected from a variety of sources and shared. Very often they need to be appropriate to a research project and may require piloting and redrafting. An agreement regarding interview-based research involving juveniles and their parents, for example, would not be worded or designed in the same way as a survey being distributed among commuters. A contract covering access to and use of commercially sensitive business data would not look the same as one seeking permission to record social interaction on a factory floor. But all such agreements have the same goal of creating a feeling of trust between researchers and human subjects.

Many funders now talk about 'informed consent agreements' and it is expected that participants should have a sufficient understanding of the project to allow them to make an informed decision about whether to contribute. However the agreement should also be written so as to defuse some of the typical problems of working with confidential data. For example security protocols for storing and accessing the data may be mentioned – even if simply undertaking to use encrypted storage. Specific variables such as name and address may be clearly mentioned as fields that will be removed from the record at some future date, or even not recorded at all. When these agreements are being drafted useful advice can often be given about whether an agreement is overly restrictive or includes unintended consequences. Is an undertaking that 'no one but the original researcher will read the interview' actually true if the intention is to send a batch of interview tapes off to a transcription service? What if excerpts are planned to be used in future articles or other publications? Promises that information being collected is only for the use of the initial research project not only prevents other academics using it later but just as importantly prevents the original researcher from using it for another research project should they wish to do so.

Experienced researchers will be accustomed to developing agreements such as these. However they may also need reminding that these arrangements now need to be appropriate not only for the initial collection and use of data but also for its long-term viability as an archived academic resource. In some ways the formal consent that is developed can reveal a great deal about the attitudes of researchers to sharing and preserving their data. Are they data miners? (The data are mine, all mine!) Discussion and education about re-use of datasets as part of the scholarly communication process can help.

Ideally, informed consent documents are drafted and agreed at the start of a project. Like DMPs they should be seen as foundational documents, which shape how the research progresses and develops. However in the real world they can equally be drafted after a project has begun or when data have already been partially collected and their value is finally recognized. Some agreements may be developed ad hoc or even put together in the closing stages of a project simply as an attempt to comply with requests for such documentation. To be asked for advice on consent agreements at any stage of a project is preferable to not being asked. So a data librarian should be prepared to provide feedback and see their value as a way of establishing contact with a research project.

Criticisms of informed consent

Sometimes the informed consent approach is criticized for being too bureaucratic or difficult to apply in practice. Some researchers cite examples of traditional methodological approaches which cannot use formal consent agreements, such as participant observation in which a degree of undercover observation is required. Other examples of situations where it could be difficult to gain informed consent from participants are when researchers are working with groups on the fringes of society, in dangerous situations such as domestic violence (Smyth and Williamson, 2004, 198), or with people from less literate cultures. So there may well be instances in which a formal approach to gaining participants' consent is burdensome or inappropriate to a particular research project. Professor Lynn Jamieson explains some of the challenges in getting written consent right for a specific research project in a YouTube video (www.youtube.com/watch?v=M0tRSQx-cfQ).

Such decisions provide another opportunity for data librarians to offer advice and comment. Informed consent means the researcher must communicate the consequences of participation in the most appropriate way, either verbally or written, immediately or perhaps later on after a rapport has been established. The ethical imperative for informed consent has to do with the notion of not harming the research subject or participants studied. A decision not to use informed consent at all may be illegal, unethical or both, and would normally be decided before a project begins, by either a departmental ethics committee or an institutional review board. However it will have important implications for data sharing, and even data storage where data protection or privacy legislation applies.

The consent agreement should be examined critically because it is a tool that protects not only respondents but also researchers. Advice and feedback about it can shape the framework it establishes for working with data, what will be seen as confidential or sensitive, and how data will be managed. It has to be acknowledged that some areas of research will always present serious confidentiality issues, some so insurmountable that closure or destruction of the data would be the only solution. The point is that this should be seen as a last and least desirable option rather than as a default starting position.

At this stage one may itemize some of the elements that define a good consent agreement and help counter criticism of overly bureaucratic documents. Ideally they should:

- be easy to understand by researcher and participant
- establish rules or conditions where contributions will and will not be used
- not be overly restrictive
- create trust
- be open to further refinement in early pilot or draft phases
- allow for changes in research practice during the data collection phase
- clarify which aspects of the data are confidential
- produce data that are usable
- produce data that are stored, preserved and sharable (in whole or in part)
- describe how the completed agreements and other documentation will be managed and stored.

Storing and preserving confidential data effectively

One of the functions of a data librarian can be to advise on key areas such as data storage. This may be covered by training delivered to early career researchers but it should not be assumed that experienced researchers always have these issues under control:

> A study of 56 professors at five American universities found that a majority had little understanding of principles, well known in the field of data curation, informing the ongoing administration of digital materials and chose to manage and store work-related data by relying on the use of their own storage devices and cloud accounts. It also found that a majority of them had experienced the loss of at least one work-related digital object that they considered to be important in the course of their professional career.
> (Schumacher and VandeCreek, 2015, 96)

It is also a common assumption that all the relevant advice will come from an IT section rather than library-based services. In reality there are a number of day-to-day practical questions that can be addressed, which are not particularly technical but rather an expression of general data management principles:

- Are data routinely encrypted or password protected?
- When sensitive data are accessed over a wi-fi network is it via a secure connection?
- Are copies of data version controlled and only created when really essential thereby avoiding unnecessary proliferation?
- Are data being stored on a standalone PC or a network server?
- Will data be transported in a secure way and how?
- If confidential parts of a data collection are to be deleted how will this be done without undue loss of non-confidential data?

The need to move data around and transport it from location to location is a useful example. Movement of data has been greatly influenced by the development of cloud computing. Services such as Dropbox have become very commonly used since they can be synchronized very easily across different computers and are a very convenient solution to the problem of moving data from one system to another. However in the case of confidential data there are a number of concerns about the reliability of such services. Debates about the legality of how data storage was evolving also led to the eventual replacement of one convention – the 'safe harbor' framework (www.theguardian.com/technology/2015/oct/06/safe-harbour-european-court-declare-invalid-data-protection) – with one called EU-US Privacy Shield. Other concerns include the potential for disclosure of a cloud service by a member of staff, or a security failure in the system. The answer perhaps is to recognize that cloud services need to be used with caution where confidential data are concerned. In particular they may be used as an effective transportation mechanism to move data around but not as a place of long-term storage.

Researchers often consider the issue of data storage only in terms of volume. This bucket approach to storage concentrates on capacity and little else. A research project may be collecting statistical survey data that will be counted in megabytes. Alternatively it may be concerned with geospatial imaging and count its data in terabytes, so planning to store appropriate volumes of material is of course important. However the principles of RDM demonstrate how storage should also concern itself with wider issues such as access, version-control, security and future preservation of data. In working with sensitive data these issues take on an added importance as they interact with questions of heightened security and trust.

Storage needs to be appropriate for the needs of the researcher compiling the data, but it also needs to go beyond that and be appropriate to the expectations of participants. For example, consider our earlier discussion of the importance of consent forms and their completion, which should make clear the researcher's intentions. Secure storage of the consent forms – usually signed by individual participants – also needs to be considered. Once signed, they need to be kept as long as the data are in existence – especially if some respondents have added special caveats. They cannot be anonymized or kept with the data so arrangements have to be arranged to keep them and protect them from unsuitable access.

Ethics committees traditionally play an important function in protecting the interests of respondents involved in research. In some disciplines, such as medicine and bio-science, ethics committees may still have a preference for data destruction as the most robust method of ensuring protection for research participants. This should be examined in detail. In fact pro-preservation researchers will find natural allies in data archivists and others involved in data management in disputing requests to destroy data as they can often supply case studies or successful scenarios for data retention. This can be seen as another potential role for data librarians in shaping institutional responses to the still sometimes contradictory expectations of data governance and management.

Data librarians need to study national legislation and regulations such as the Health Insurance Portability and Accountability Act of 1996 (HIPPA) in the USA, which provides data privacy and security provisions for safeguarding medical information, and data protection legislation in Europe, which gives rights to individuals regarding the data that are collected about them by government and other bodies, and advise researchers accordingly. Individual countries have up to date resources that can be consulted, and options for training to become more informed.

DEALING WITH SENSITIVE DATA   131

Approaches to anonymizing confidential and sensitive data

Are there common tactics in dealing with these issues where advice is needed? One tactic is to attempt anonymization, which is also an example of when worst case scenario planning can be useful. Confidential data gathered during research often has to undergo some editing to remove identifying information, and researchers frequently seek advice on the positive and negative aspects of anonymization, especially if data are to be preserved and made available for potential re-use by others. However excessive use of over-anonymization, especially for qualitative data, can be an issue: there is little point putting effort into preserving and archiving a dataset that has been rendered meaningless because too much content has been removed. It may no longer contain sensitive data but it has also been degraded as an academic resource. The goal is to achieve an appropriate balance between protecting respondents' privacy and meeting expectations about data preservation and then sharing data with researchers and other stakeholders. The two risks are tightly bound up together.

Research councils and funding bodies have begun to argue for the preservation of research data rather than destroying them for a variety of reasons. The preservation of research data allows replication and verification of research analysis and is a deterrent against research fraud. Curating data so they remain re-usable into the future allows them to be re-analysed with new techniques or combined with other data collections to create fresh findings. A great deal of data represent information that cannot easily be collected again because of their cost or nature. For example, political opinion data collected one week before an election cannot be recreated if they are lost by conducting the same poll one week after the election. With the increased appreciation of the long-term value in research data any technique that dulls or degrades them has to be employed with care.

There are degrees of anonymization to be considered. For quantitative data simple aggregation may be used in many cases and it is an effective method. Categories may be collapsed so, for example, a detailed occupation scheme is recoded into a higher order classification such as social grade. However such techniques lead to loss of detail in the data and many researchers are beginning to recognize that such valuable content needs to be retained. This is why non-aggregated survey data or microdata have long been preserved in data archives and promoted as a resource. Data creators often begin with an overly draconian view of how they need to edit their data to make them 'anonymous and safe'. A high degree of content is removed when in fact a 'light touch' approach may be more than enough. Choices will of course depend on the nature of the data and how they are structured. For example when anonymizing quantitative and geospatial data, researchers may remove identifying variables and generalize, or aggregate geographies into areas of larger populations. Personal identifiers can be replaced with randomized case identifiers.

In research projects in which qualitative or multimedia data have been collected researchers should be encouraged to leave content alone as much as possible. Editing should focus on that which is easily defined and limited in nature. In many cases the best advice follows a consultation or meeting about the specific nature and issues of a data collection. Also, as has been noted, 'No matter how clear the guidance, people will always want to pick up the phone and ask someone how it relates to them' (Ward et al., 2011, 269). So the ability to arrange consultations will always be in demand. Anonymization is an area where effective data management services can be promoted not as top-down guidance but as a forum for discussion and consultation about best handling of the data.

Opportunities to share a wider variety of research data

A more detailed consideration of issues of confidentiality and anonymization allows a greater variety of data to be preserved. It is possible to point to examples of audiovisual data now being routinely archived and re-used. At one time this would have been seen as impossible because of general concerns about confidentiality. The assumption would have been that while a transcription from an audio recorded interview or meeting could be edited and prepared for re-use after analysis, the actual recording remains problematic and should therefore be destroyed. Audio data, like video, represent a valuable resource that should be preserved whenever consent agreements and legal and ethical considerations make it possible, even if the original research team who created the material have little use for it themselves once transcriptions have been produced. Applications of some of the principles of data management and preservation have opened up this type of data to wider use. Changes in attitudes and practices are discussed in 'Is This Thing Working? – The challenge of digital audio for qualitative research' (Southall, 2009).

Preparation of audiovisual data for preservation and re-use is helped if problematic sections are removed, but this is time consuming. Other approaches such as pitch-shifting or distorting the sound of the audio may be suggested but these are really examples of over-anonymization, in which the data are being degraded, distorted and eroded. More detailed planning in how consent is worded and how interviews are structured can be much more useful in allowing the effective preservation of a dataset. For example, pre-arranged clear procedures can be agreed for signalling off-the-record comments so that recording would pause if the speaker realizes they are about to reveal disclosive information, such as personal details about family members or work colleagues, they had not originally intended mentioning. Use of pseudonyms agreed in advance and used in the audio recording, rather than added later, during transcription, as is traditionally the case, is another example. In this way early thought about who will use the data creates a framework that influences decisions about editing and anonymization.

Protecting data while making it accessible

Anonymization is a limited tool, most appropriate to quantitative or geospatial data. If used on qualitative data it can be easily overused and detrimental to data quality and the ability to replicate research, but alternative approaches to allowing use of confidential data in appropriate ways are becoming more popular. For example, mechanisms allowing access to preserved data can be used creatively. Providing access to data by request or restricting access are the basic options that most archives and repositories are able to offer. However researchers may also be encouraged to think in terms of linking use of confidential data to restricted access – available only to registered users or to a specific type of user (academic, non-commercial researcher, approved institution etc.). Stronger access options include vetting of future users by data depositors or nominated data stewards, setting conditions about how collections may be used and cited, or creating time-limited embargoes. Education, guidance and promotion of these options are key tasks of a data librarian. Anonymization, summarization and aggregation of data may be the first suggestions made by researchers considering sharing their data but the creative use of access restrictions can be even more effective in maintaining confidentiality and quality of data collections.

Thinking creatively about access and embargo periods allows particularly sensitive datasets to be preserved and made available for re-use within boundaries. An embargo may be set for a limited period and can be useful if content is time sensitive. The collection is deposited and therefore preserved but access is not possible until a specified time. There may be issues around the management of such an embargo as in some cases it may create more administrative work. For example if an open-ended embargo is used (where an end date is to be negotiated at a future date) there could be problems of finally agreeing access. This is an argument for avoiding open-ended embargoes. The depositor may become uncontactable or simply refuse to be pinned down and specify an end date. In practice it is better to decide at point of deposit when an embargo will end.

Although more management of a collection may be involved, one advantage of using agreed embargo periods is that it is useful for datasets where general content is creating concerns over confidentiality. It may be proving difficult to take a light touch anonymization approach. So the emphasis is shifted away from what has to be done to a collection to make it safe or suitable for use. Instead the concern becomes one of how it is going to be accessed and how that particular stage of the research lifecycle can be structured to protect confidentiality. Restricted access conditions or an agreed embargo act to limit who will use the data and can be suggested as safeguards to prevent unintended disclosure of confidential information. This approach is used by suppliers of economic microdata such as Statistics Canada or Eurostat. The procedure used by the latter involves researchers applying for access well in advance and providing a full account of their methodology and research question. Everyone who will come into contact with the data needs to be identified and approved and plans for storage and use clearly agreed. For example, the secure data lab of the UK Data Service uses a procedure where a researcher has to be given approved status as part of an application. An account of the intended methodology and research question is once again required.

Making sensitive data shareable

One approach to making restricted data accessible and shareable is based on the 'Five safes of data' (see Table 8.1), a framework 'for designing, describing and evaluating access systems for data, used by data providers, data users, and regulators. The model integrates analysis of opportunities, constraints, costs and benefits of different approaches, taking account of the level of data anonymization, the likely users, the scope for training, the environment through which data are accessed, and the statistical outputs derived from data use' (Desai, Ritchie and Welpton, 2016, 3).

Table 8.1 *The five 'safes' of data*

Safe projects	Is this use of the data appropriate?
Safe people	Can the researchers be trusted to use it in an appropriate manner?
Safe data	Is there a disclosure risk in the data itself?
Safe settings	Does the access facility limit unauthorized use?
Safe outputs	Are the statistical results non-disclosive?
The concept of the five safes is from UKDA; see, for example, blog.ukdataservice.ac.uk/access-to-sensitive-data-for-research-the-5-safes.	

These access risks, or issues of data safety, are derived from best practice for secure data access established internationally by organizations such as the UK Office for National Statistics Virtual Microdata Laboratory and the NORC Data Enclave at University of Chicago (www.norc.org, an independent American research organization).

Much of what has been discussed in this chapter demonstrates the need to balance commitments to protecting confidentiality and commitments to creating – or encouraging the creation of – preserved and re-usable data collections. This can sometimes be very difficult and where the two are in direct opposition the needs of the former will always be paramount. However the advice and support provided through any RDM infrastructure should seek to minimize occasions where direct opposition occurs. Assumptions that confidential or sensitive data always present insurmountable difficulties when being considered for preservation, archiving or sharing must not be permitted. Instead the key message should be that problems regarding confidentiality can be overcome in many cases through careful planning.

Key take-away points
- Researchers can easily overestimate problems of handling and sharing confidential or sensitive data.
- Stakeholder encouragement of increased data preservation can conflict with expectations of data destruction by other stakeholders.
- Where sensitive content is specific and particular it can be removed in a process of anonymization.
- Data librarians can offer a fresh viewpoint on data and put concerns about breaches of confidentiality into proper perspective.
- Consent agreements not only define a framework for understanding research participant's wishes but also how the data should be used and managed after they have been collected.
- Providing advice and feedback on draft consent agreements can be a useful way of establishing contact with active researchers in early stages of a project.
- Secure data storage should also be concerned with wider issues such as access, version-control and future preservation.
- Advice will need to be congruent or even integrated with existing institutional procedures of research ethical review.
- In some cases sensitive data may be better preserved and better protected by restricting access or embargo than by anonymization.

Reflective questions
1. Are there categories of data which will always be too confidential or sensitive to be preserved? What are the reasons and could they change?
2. What mechanisms and information might you develop to help researchers assess concerns in this area?
3. Should advice focus on specific parts of the data that are troublesome that

could be easily removed?
4. Will the data be degraded or distorted if content is removed?
5. Why do researchers respond better to case studies or real world scenarios than to guidelines on handling data?
6. Are there typical issues or concerns in your discipline where it would be useful to develop scenarios and case studies that illustrate solutions?
7. What repositories or other options are currently available to your discipline for preserving sensitive research data?

CHAPTER 9
Data sharing in the disciplines

Culture change in academia

To work in research support is to be immersed in culture change, sometimes fast, sometimes slow. The arrival of a killer app or new technology may seem to transform the way research is conducted in a given field very quickly. On the other hand, universities have existed for centuries, and knowledge and research know-how are passed on from teacher to student in time-honoured fashion. Tradition slows down culture change, and minimizes effects of external factors on researchers' behaviour, such as the use of social media.

For example, young researchers who may not think twice about sharing aspects of their private life on social media may learn to be very guarded about revealing their data. This may be the case if their discipline's norms are to consider data to be a kind of capital, on which to fashion one's career. This is not wholly bad in itself, because it may protect them from jeopardizing their chances of getting published – for which an original work is usually required. Indeed, the Belmont Forum's Open Data Survey found that younger researchers were more concerned about being able to publish results before releasing data than older researchers (Schmidt, Gemeinholzer and Treloar, 2016, 6–7).

So we tend to find that innovations in scholarly communication can take a generation or more to take root. For this reason librarians are often in the difficult position of championing scholarly innovations to research communities that seem stubbornly resistant to change. In these circumstances it can be challenging to find the right balance of patience and initiative. A support network of peers within your institution or in the wider world is therefore highly recommended!

In the social sciences

In our first chapter we discussed the history of data libraries and data archives, and the strong economic motivation of social scientists for getting access to large-scale survey and population census data collected by government agencies. The prevalence of data sharing for social scientists then are often focused on the receiving end of sharing. Large-scale academic surveys and longitudinal studies, known to be rich sources for re-use and funded with an expectation they will become resources for the wider community, are an exception. Perhaps it is human nature to appreciate the receiving part of sharing more than the giving? This is a common theme of studies on attitudes towards sharing and openness in academic culture (for example, Tenopir et al., 2015). So in the social sciences we find that re-use of data has always been valued.

Verification of findings, replication of results, which are part of the scientific method, has perhaps been less valued. Therefore, social scientists had not acquired the habit of sharing small-scale or one-off surveys and interviews, because the re-use value was considered low and this is one of the features of long tail data, introduced in Chapter 2. Any interesting findings may be fully mined in one or two papers by the data creators. Replicating someone else's findings has not offered enough tangible reward for it to be common, with the exception perhaps of a tradition in economics of attempting to replicate published journal articles in class assignments for undergraduates and postgraduates.

In practice however replication exercises can pay off: Thomas Herndon, a 28 year old PhD student at the University of Massachusetts (UMass) Amherst made worldwide headlines by debunking a renowned study on which government policies had been based. The student requested underlying data by e-mail from the Harvard co-authors of the 2010 study, 'Growth in a Time of Debt', which provided evidence that high levels of debt consistently impeded the growth of national economies. The study laid the basis for the Austerity Movement in the wake of the 2008 global recession, including that embraced by the UK Conservative coalition government, European Union leaders and Republican critics of the Obama administration. The authors eventually e-mailed Herndon the dataset, and he found that key data had been omitted in a formula the spreadsheet used. Once he convinced his supervisor that he was correct and that Reinhart and Rogoff's analysis of their own dataset was wrong, they were able to quickly publish a paper disputing the original results, which was in line with good research practice but caused an uproar in the press and among policy circles (Roose, 2013).

Psychology, on the other hand, which relies in part on small, experimental datasets, has lacked a strong tradition of verification or data sharing. Data archivists at DANS in the Netherlands documented the absence of good data management and sharing practices in a study of Dutch academic psychologists in 2010: 'Even though their opinions may differ widely, most psychologists would not even consider making their data available for verification or a second opinion by a colleague or outsider. Besides this, much of the data gets lost over the course of time because no clear rules exist for archiving data within the profession' (Doorn, Dillo and van Horik, 2013, 230). This argument was supported the next year when the Stapel Affair came to light, the first of three major scientific fraud cases to emerge in the Netherlands in 2011–12:

> The social psychologist Diederik Stapel was an influential professor until a group of young researchers, on the basis of outcomes which they considered 'too good to be true', smelt a rat. In the final report, which was recently published by a committee that evaluated all of Stapel's work at the universities of Tilburg, Groningen and Amsterdam, it is now clear that 55 of his publications are based on fictitious data.
>
> (Doorn, Dillo and van Horik, 2013, 2)

Two high-level reports resulted from the fraud cases, stressing scientific integrity and the need for scrupulous academic behaviour. One of the reports highlighted the riskiness of small science practice involving a lone researcher, as opposed to research teams of big science where protocols for data management and checking of each other's work is more likely to occur (Doorn, Dillo and van Horik, 2013, 3).

So can psychology change its closed data culture? The authors of the Dutch paper noted that other disciplines without a data sharing tradition, such as archaeology, were able to change quickly when confronted with logical arguments, and especially funder requirements. Between 2007 and 2013, 19,000 digital archaeological datasets were collected for archiving and re-use, inspired by the success of the Archaeological Data Service in the UK; 'As an excavation can be carried out only once, archaeologists now generally recognize the need for a digital archive' (Doorn, Dillo and van Horik, 2013, 12).

In the sciences

What about data sharing in the physical, biological and medical scientific disciplines? Each has its own contradictions, and practice varies by country, sub-discipline and institutional environment. There is a small but growing literature examining evidence of data sharing culture in a range of settings. This is even beginning to show change over time (and in a positive direction), though perceived 'risks' and barriers persist (Tenopir et al., 2015).

Astronomy is recognized as a leader in open data sharing, having tackled its big data crisis early and using shared international digital infrastructures for both collection and analysis. This is why a vignette from this field was a valuable contribution to Chapter 6. Like many other physical sciences, confidentiality about human subjects is not an issue; unlike some of them, neither is commercial application (patents). Perhaps because of their leadership in developing global data infrastructures, as with the Sloan Digital Sky Survey, and their long association with amateur enthusiasts, aka citizen scientists, astronomy has been one of the earliest fields to use crowd-sourcing technology effectively. A good example can be seen in Galaxy Zoo. As noted on the SDSS website, 'Galaxy Zoo (www.galaxyzoo.org) launched in 2007 to deal with the one million images in the SDSS Main Galaxy Sample. It is now the most productive citizen science project in existence, and this success spawned a "Zooniverse" of other citizen science projects across all areas of science' (www.sdss.org/education).

Generally, disciplines that rely on large, international collaborations can more easily make the switch to sharing openly. But disciplines like particle physics, which generates data from shared facilities such as the Large Hadron Collider at CERN (which produces 15 petabytes of data per year), have trouble identifying what should sensibly be shared publicly. A 2013 case study of the Particle Physics and Particle Astrophysics Group at the University of Sheffield in England, by the RECODE project, explained:

> This case provides insights into values and motivations that shape the collecting, disseminating, storing and processing large quantities of numerical data from experiments which have hundreds of academic partners. Before recording the raw data, it is pre-processed to reduce the number of events from around 40 million per second to 200 per second. It highlights some of the barriers because even with this reduction, making the data publicly available is questionable – the resources necessary for storing and processing the data are only available to very large consortia.
>
> (Sveinsdottir et al., 2013, 16)

Unlike in astronomy, perhaps there can be no such thing as an amateur particle physicist. The physicists interviewed in the RECODE study believe the ability to extract meaningful information from the data requires years of education and training. Some felt the only sensible way to provide public access to their data was through specially prepared teaching materials. The ATLAS project, for example, included an outreach deliverable, which involved preparing, processing and annotating a small proportion of the data by a full-time member of staff. We would argue that information professionals need to be aware of these domain-based variations when offering relevant support and advice on data management. Guidance on ways of preserving research data would have little appeal for physicists who feel that scaling this type of work up to produce large amounts of 'open data' would be a waste of public monies. They would consider it more appropriate to fund the experiments themselves and the research outcomes from them (Sveinsdottir et al., 2013, 62).

The physicists interviewed in the RECODE study thought that sharing with other physicists outside collaborative teams was sometimes useful, e.g. to compare experimental results with different calibrations, but much communication was necessary to ensure even highly trained physicists did not misinterpret others' results. Moreover, there is a competitive aspect to the great discoveries of physics such as the Higgs Boson, dark matter particles and gravitational waves, which discourages openness among teams at early stages of research.

Clinical health is a field fraught with data-sharing issues, leading to strong contradictory tendencies for both opening up and restricting data access, resulting sometimes in some very complicated data governance arrangements. A role for the data librarian lies in being aware of these and promoting the benefits of data sharing wherever possible. According to another RECODE case study, 'Our respondents stated clear benefits of both sharing and opening access to data, in the sense that . . . having access to more research would lead to faster advancement within the field, and results would become more reliable, as they can be drawn from a bigger pool of data' (Sveinsdottir et al., 2013, 63). Other benefits of data sharing to note, particularly with regard to clinical studies, include overcoming what is known as publication bias, or publishing only when a significant result is found, and reducing patient burden and duplication of effort. The first is a huge issue when so much research in the discipline depends on meta-analyses (combining results of a number of individual studies). If negative results are routinely not published, then positive results can be over-emphasized. Also the same research is at risk of being repeated needlessly if negative results go unpublished. Concern about this runs deep, because of the potential to reduce patient suffering if the trend can be reversed.

Is data sharing a solution to publication bias? Stakeholders – in addition to the researchers, their funders, their publishers and would-be data re-users – complicate the scene in clinical health research: the pharmaceutical industry tends to view data as commercially sensitive, and patients could be unwilling to share their data because of privacy concerns. Added to this are the various issues already discussed in Chapter 8: legal and ethical issues around handling personal and sensitive data, the nature of informed consent, the difficulty of ensuring data are truly anonymized, and data protection (privacy) legislation, making the sharing of clinical health data a minefield of explosive and costly potential mistakes. In combination these factors keep the field quite conservative with regard to data sharing, despite the enormity of the potential benefits.

Recall that in Chapter 7 we discussed four ways of managing access to archived data: open, managed, secure and closed. In practice open data sharing rarely occurs with clinical data. Instead, more or less formal systems of application and vetting take place, which aim to ensure that data remain in safe hands only, but that can cause extremely inconvenient time delays in gaining access to datasets. Chapter 8 dealt with ways of sharing data that are potentially sensitive through various options including confidentiality agreements; depending on the requirements of the agreement and support available to the user to understand and meet them, this may involve more delays before a research question can be answered. Until data sharing in this field becomes more standardized, research involving re-use of clinical data will be frustrating, to say the least. Some feel that at this stage it is more strategic to ensure that the existence of a given clinical trial can be known, rather than to advocate data sharing with its many obstacles; see for example, the AllTrials campaign (www.alltrials.net; Goldacre, 2015).

The field of biological sciences has a number of standards and established shared services for recording and sharing data (gene, protein and other structured databases). The Human Genome Project was an early example of international scientific collaboration and data sharing for the greater good, leading to an open resource on the world wide web instead of a corporately owned patent:

> Indeed, one of the early principles agreed upon by leaders of the Human Genome Project was that the DNA sequence generated should be freely available to the public. This principle was codified in the 1997 Bermuda Principles, which set forth the expectation that all DNA sequence information should be released into publicly available databases within 24 hours of being generated. This policy of open access to the genome has been a core ethos of genomics ever since. . . . In a landmark decision in June 2013, the Supreme Court determined that DNA in its natural form cannot be patented.
>
> (www.genome.gov/19016590, 2014)

As with chemistry, which has some exemplary established practices, such as crystallography databases, there are contradictions within the fields of biological sciences in its concern about the ability to commercialize research, e.g. through patents, and old-fashioned data hoarding based on the 'working capital' argument (Williams et al., 2009) – that researchers' data are their working capital, on which they may choose to study and publish findings throughout their lifetime.

The environmental sciences produce huge amounts of observational data (which by their nature cannot be reproduced), some of which are shared, curated and integrated through large data centres, observatories and agencies, much of which is openly accessible. For example, the website of the Intergovernmental Panel on Climate Change's Data Distribution Centre (www.ipcc-data.org) provides data observations, simulations and visualizations. Climate change is a scientific pursuit that is very much in the public eye. The discipline also makes great use of citizen science data collection technologies, for topics ranging from bird-watching to monitoring Dutch Elm disease. Yet one recent paper in the field of ecology laments that much ecological research produces 'dark data', or data that are not shared. This is mainly because other than a few expensive big science projects, most studies are small, and researchers simply publish findings and move on to the next project without preserving or sharing their data. This is typical of long tail data. In this field, 'Ecologists collectively produce large volumes of data through diverse individual projects but lack a culture of data curation and sharing, so that ecological data are missing from the landscape of data-intensive science' (Hampton et al., 2013, 156). However, Hampton and his co-authors note recent exceptions to this rule, such as the DataOne Federation funded by the NSF, and the Dryad data repository, which archives datasets on behalf of journals in evolutionary biology and related fields and encourages ecologists to make their hand-crafted data available to 'plug and play' in the larger stream of data, such as those managed by earth observatories.

In arts and humanities

Perhaps no scientific discipline is without its data sharing contradictions. The arts and humanities have some large, well funded, highly co-ordinated research projects that break new ground in their technological innovations, but more common are numerous, small and unfunded research projects, which have no stakeholder requirements for data management planning and lack any tradition of data sharing. These present opportunities for data librarians to develop contacts with ongoing projects and discuss the benefits of data management and data sharing.

As we remarked in Chapter 2 assumptions about what constitutes data can vary and it is in the arts and humanities where you may have to address the question, 'What are data, in the context of my research?' In this area data can be photographs, correspondence and other works, anything that influences research outputs. These outputs take many forms and are often represented by a digital surrogate – such as a recording of a dance performance or a 3D visual representation of a sculpture. These data assets are as much at risk of being lost as any other discipline, perhaps more, since there is not a pre-existing concept of data to be managed.

Some humanities fields such as history have a strong tradition and understanding around the use of primary resources such as archival manuscripts and secondary resources, such as newspapers. It is largely down to staff in archives and libraries to manage such resources on behalf of these researchers, including through digitization programmes and catalogues, as well as ongoing conservation (for analogue objects) and digital preservation. But the rise of digital humanities is creating large numbers of highly creative and tailored websites and tools, which are in danger of being lost soon after the project funding runs out. A recent project at the University of Oxford with the humanities division found numerous cases of this phenomenon and productive links with the library were established. The cases were not just from early career researchers but sometimes were ongoing web-based projects founded decades ago.

Web archiving can only be part of the solution, as this works best for static (not dynamic) web pages, also known as the 'deep web' – resources in databases which web crawlers cannot access, or are prohibited from accessing. Where there are valued digital assets stored within the websites, such as cultural heritage objects, one solution may be to store them with as much metadata as possible in repositories with persistent identifiers, and let the website with its bells and whistles fall into neglect as the funding for maintenance eventually disappears. This at least is one way for researchers to address the sustainability requirement of funders, though it may not excite them to store their digital objects in such a plain vanilla envelope. Another is to try to store the code of the website for the long term, so that it could in future be rebuilt, given enough interest. A virtual machine image may be captured for the same reason. Potentially standardization can help with longevity of the products of digital humanities, both metadata and ontologies, but also the creation of databases using RDF and XML, which lend themselves to being queried by multiple languages.

This attempt at describing the contradictions about data sharing in many disciplines may seem overly generalized for those knowledgeable about a given discipline or sub-discipline. Certainly it represents only a snapshot of a gradually changing reality. Hopefully all of these disciplines are increasingly valuing the role of data management, publication, archiving and sharing in the sense of both giving and taking. These changes, albeit occurring at different rates in different disciplines, demonstrate that substantial progress is being made. There is a demand for information professionals to get involved and make a difference, which makes the field of academic data curation and support an exciting one for data librarians.

Key take-away points
- Innovations can take a generation or more to take root in culture, especially academic culture, which is steeped in tradition.
- Astronomy has been an early innovator in citizen science and crowd-sourcing tools, the advent of Galaxy Zoo for the Sloan Digital Sky Survey being a case in point.
- Registries of clinical trials and their protocols are seen as a way towards more openness in clinical health compensating for the numerous difficulties arising from data sharing in the field.
- The Human Genome Project was an early example of organized data sharing for the greater good in biological sciences.
- Use of standards (for metadata, ontologies, databases) in the digital humanities can go a long way towards making digital resources produced in research projects sustainable for the future.

Reflective questions
1. Why might younger early career researchers be more concerned about open data sharing than older more established ones?
2. What lessons do economics, psychology and archaeology provide for shedding light on data sharing in the social sciences?
3. What challenges and successes can you identify for data sharing in the physical sciences?
4. What does 'dark data' have to do with the 'publication bias'?
5. How might you adapt your language and concepts for communicating with an arts researcher about data management and sharing?

CHAPTER 10
Supporting open scholarship and open science

The notable rise in the perceived value of data sharing across disciplines at the present time, as demonstrated in Chapter 9, probably has two distinct origins, which influence disciplines in tandem: the open access movement in its broadest sense; and data science, with its roots in computational methods and its embrace of the 'data revolution' (Hey, Tansley and Tolle, 2009). Both of these are having a positive and potentially powerful effect on data sharing and re-use. In this chapter we draw evidence from the broader area of scholarly communication in order to bring the discourse about the nature of data librarianship right up to the present, and peer into a possible future – one where technologies may be harnessed in ways that lead to an acceleration of not just data accumulation but knowledge creation and dissemination. This would benefit not just scientists and scholars but – through increased transparency and accessibility – potentially the full range of human endeavours. Concepts discussed in this chapter in particular may be usefully explored using the Open Research Glossary (www.righttoresearch.org/resources/OpenResearchGlossary) for those unfamiliar with them.

Going green: impact of the open access movement

The primary reasons for and against open access to digital content can be summed up in this famous quote by Stewart Brand, creator of the *Whole Earth Catalog* and The WELL, an early internet community network based in San Francisco: 'Information wants to be free – because it is now so easy to copy and distribute casually – and information wants to be expensive – because in an Information Age, nothing is so valuable as the right information at the right time.' The quote has been attributed to Brand at the first Hackers Conference, 1984 (www.rogerclarke.com/II/IWtbF.html).

This summarizes the conflict between those who wish to access information over the internet at the click of a button without paying for it and those who wish to build paywalls around commodified information products for profit. Libraries normally help users get over paywalls simply by paying for access to digital content on behalf of a community, sometimes getting the price lowered through negotiation, consortia-building, buying products in bundles and building collections as discussed in Chapter 4.

Since about the turn of the last century, however, in addition to arguments made about fairness in access to information for developing countries and other poorer communities, academic libraries have simply struggled to pay the bills for the journals in demand by their readers, leading to the open access movement as we know it. How did this come about?

Various trends have caused a crisis in the traditional model of scholarly publishing and access through libraries. Costs of production may be lower for digital publications than print; costs of creation and peer review are in effect donated to publishers by the academic community. In this model academics sign over their copyright to publishers who have exclusive rights to re-use the material in other publications, or sell licences to those who wish to do so – sometimes back to the authors themselves; this model is increasingly perceived as dysfunctional. The increasing consolidation of titles held by publisher behemoths, the lack of any realistic cap on prices for journals with high-impact factors, limitations on ever-increasing library acquisition budgets, and the sheer proliferation of published output coupled with rising expectations of access have all made the traditional model seem untenable. Legislative copyright reforms that have benefited corporate copyright-holders disproportionately over individual content creators and users have helped to create a situation where piracy has become commonplace and is sometimes regarded as heroic, especially when benefiting many. All of these issues have a bearing on the landscape of RDM and the work of data librarians.

Libraries, universities, academics as authors and academics as readers find themselves increasingly swept up in the tide of the open access movement, which aims to correct the situation through different methods. 'Green' open access allows a content creator to retain rights to their work even when published through a traditional mechanism; normally this includes depositing a copy in one's institutional repository, after an embargo period if required by the publisher. 'Gold' open access means the publishers make their money by charging authors rather than readers; where this is encouraged, most institutions provide publishing fees on behalf of academic staff, sometimes with contributions from research funders.

Clearly, publishers add much value to the publishing process, but some question if the price (particularly for high-impact journals) is justified, especially when the peer review process is largely donated labour from academics. Some not-for-profit gold publishers have emerged that aim to keep publishing costs low, arguing that publishers have an inflated stake in the value chain and that academics would be better off publishing their own output (notably PLoS). Other publishers provide hybrid journals where the author has a choice whether to pay or be paid for their articles. In some countries, such as the UK, the research reward system is being tinkered with so that only open access publications may be allowed for consideration in the UK's 2020 REF – which determines funding levels passed from government to individual institutions, and has a great impact on individual research careers.

We would argue that it must be the case that the movement towards open access publication will have a knock-on effect of increased data sharing, as the culture changes from a view of scholarly publication as commodity for profit to one of expected sharing and easy access. However in the short term all data librarians can do is continue to highlight the benefits to researchers of managing and preserving data – whether being shared as open or restricted access.

Free software, open data and data licences

Open access is used in relation to literature, but the first advocates of openness were computer scientists. Richard Stallman, who worked as a programmer at MIT in the 1970s, started the free software movement. 'Free as in speech, not free as in beer' is a common explanation of this principle, based on the early hackers' (programmers') culture of swapping and altering code at will to make better software. Stallman resisted the move towards making software proprietary because it forbade the sharing and alteration of code, which he regarded as an affront against natural human co-operation, rather than because of the pricetag that comes with it.

In his 1985 GNU (Gnu Not Unix) Manifesto, Stallman said:

> I consider that the golden rule requires that if I like a program I must share it with other people who like it. Software sellers want to divide the users and conquer them, making each user agree not to share with others. I refuse to break solidarity with other users in this way. I cannot in good conscience sign a non-disclosure agreement or a software license agreement.
>
> (http://wikiquote.org/wiki/Richard_Stallman)

By creating a version of the Unix operating system licensed by his GNU General Public Licence, still commonly used, Stallman could ensure that free software had a platform that was not only free but constantly improved by a community of like-minded programmers. In this way he invented the concept of 'copyleft', the opposite of copyright, because it encourages sharing and co-operation by requiring any further product built on the licensed code to be licensed in the same way – e.g. not made proprietary.

So the concept of 'information wants to be free' has been a strong undercurrent since the beginning of the internet, and it is easy to see how it has influenced not only the open access publishing movement, but also such powerful tools as the world wide web and its free browsers dating back to Mosaic and Netscape, ad-powered search engines including the mega-successful Google, the Linux operating system (Linus Torvald's answer to Unix, for the personal computer) and other open source software, freeware, 'freemium' apps and cloud services, Web 2.0 social networks, Creative Commons licences for expressive works, and open (government) data.

Big data as a new paradigm?

Tony Hey, the Director of the UK e-Science Core Programme, wrote in 2003 about the 'data deluge', a foreshadowing of the contemporary term, big data, in a time when high performance computing infrastructure was 'on the grid' rather than 'in the cloud' (Hey and Trefethen, 2003). In 2009 Hey co-edited a volume dedicated to Jim Gray, the computing visionary based at Microsoft Research (formerly eScience group) who pioneered the idea that when datasets get large, the computer code should be brought to the data, rather than vice versa (this is now sometimes called data gravity) (Hey, Tansley and Tolle, 2009). The book, building on Gray's original ideas (in his absence because of his untimely death) proposed that science had reached a turning point, called the fourth paradigm, which goes beyond empirical observation and experimentation; beyond analytical and theoretical approaches, and even beyond computer simulation. 'Increasingly, scientific breakthroughs will be powered by advanced computing capabilities that help researchers manipulate and explore massive datasets' (Hey, Tansley and Tolle, 2009, 258). This has been an intriguing proposal for the scientific community, whether they believe the phenomenon is truly new, or not, as evidenced by one scientist's book review:

> The authors of the Fourth Paradigm book consider that the capability to do important basic science by exploring data archives is a consequence of recent advances in computer and sensor technology. I would suggest, though, that this paradigm comes into play whenever the rate of accumulation of data greatly outstrips the rate of accumulation of interpretation, i.e. the rate at which the scientific community can assimilate data into an interpretive framework. This imbalance can happen when the cost of accumulating data drops. But it can also happen when there are non-science drivers spurring the accumulation of data.
>
> (Karstens, 2012)

This view is similar to the notion that what makes big data challenging is not absolute size (or volume), but the necessity to rethink data handling and analysis, and then retool. So for a researcher who has always used a desktop PC for analysis, moving to a high performance computing environment is a significant change. For others moving from working with small Excel spreadsheets to using database queries (such as SQL or MySQL) over remotely held data may be completely new, and may require new forms of support and training from library staff. Indeed it also raises questions about the most appropriate role of libraries themselves in relation to big data.

Perhaps those who would question whether the data revolution has ushered in a new scientific paradigm are the same who feel that the attention given to big data is nothing but hype. But hype is almost by definition short lived; in Gartner's well known 'Hype Cycle' model, big data were already past the 'peak of inflated expectations' in 2014, part-way down to the 'trough of disillusionment', after which it could be expected to slowly make its way up the 'slope of enlightenment' to the 'plateau of productivity' (www.gartner.com/newsroom/id/2819918). In 2015 the term did not even appear.

Another criticism of big data is that the allure of having *all of the data*, and not needing to sample, leads to ignorance of other sorts of systemic bias in the data. In a keynote speech to the Royal Statistical Society, Tim Harford has suggested there are a number of big data traps that those lacking deep knowledge of statistics can fall into. Looking forward he suggests that statisticians embrace lessons of the past and work collaboratively with researchers of other disciplines to explore the terrain of big data (Harford, 2014).

It seems that the hard sciences are not the only ones facing paradigm changes tied up with new forms of data and toolsets. Social media streams, commercial transactional data and government administrative data are promising sources for the social sciences to explore, once they master the technological and methodological issues involved, not to mention potential restrictions on access or ethical controls. These are areas where demands for support, advice and guidance are growing all the time. Social network analysis, for example, has been a 'goldmine' for the social sciences and there has been an 'explosion of interest' in this method for over a decade (Borgatti et al., 2009).

The digital humanities are bringing order to studying large, newly digitized collections, corpora, cultural heritage objects, art and photography, multimedia and performing arts. In some cases they are using the same languages and tools (such as Python) as their scientific counterparts, in others they are inventing new standards and ontologies to organize and analyse their content. The big data problems faced by humanists were articulated by Christine Borgman, in a keynote address to a 2009 digital humanities conference:

Issues of scale are of general interest because methods and problems must be approached much differently when one has, for example, the full text of a million books rather than a handful. Inspection is no longer feasible; only computational methods can examine corpora on that scale. Issues of language and communication, which are central to the humanities, are of broader interest for problems such as pattern detection and cross-language indexing and retrieval. Space and time encompass the new research methods possible with geographic information systems, geo-tagged documents and images, and the increased ability to make temporal comparisons.

(Borgman, 2009, 10)

Data as first-class research objects

Some open data advocates argue that until data are treated as first-class research objects those who create and curate data for the benefit of research will never get due credit in the way that authors of publications, especially in high-impact factor journals, do. 'Open data can override the individual interests of the researchers who generate the data, such that novel ways of recognizing and rewarding their contribution must be developed. . . . Junior researchers, PhD students and/or technicians may be particularly vulnerable to lack of recognition, and with limited say in data reuse' (Science International, 2015, 6). Nor, they argue, will data creators have enough incentives to share their data without the kinds of benefits that writing publications give, such as the prospect of receiving numerous citations. Therefore, it is essential – as discussed in previous chapters – that people cite data properly and that data are shared in a way that enables proper citation, for example by following guidelines for producing metadata typically provided by data repositories.

So what do we know about the impact of data in science and scholarship through data citations? Not a lot, since data have been hidden behind the research literature for much of the time the scholarly record has built up. There have, however, been a few studies about the relative benefit for those who share data versus those who do not. A 2010 American study examined 'the extent to which social science research data are shared and assess[ed] whether data sharing affects research productivity tied to the research data themselves' (Pienta, Alter and Lyle, 2010, 1). The results were significant in both senses (statistically and *prima facie*): 'Archiving data lead[s] to 2.98 times more publications than not sharing data. When data are shared informally (compared to not shared at all), 2.77 times the number of publications is produced.' (One can assume in this study that all publications cited the dataset in some way because they appeared in a database about data collections sponsored by either the NSF or the NIH.)

Another study examined the 'open data citation advantage' using a large sample and controlling for known citation advantage factors: 'In a multivariate regression on 10,555 studies that created gene expression microarray data, we found that studies that made data available in a public repository received 9% . . . more citations than similar studies for which the data [were] not made available' (Piwowar and Vision, 2013, 1). In astronomy, an advantage was found for citations of papers with explicit links to data: 'Articles with links to data result in higher citation rates than articles without such links' (Henneken and Accomazzi, 2011, 1). More specifically, 'articles with data links on average acquired 20% more citations (compared to articles without these links) over a period of 10 years' (Henneken and Accomazzi, 2011, 2).

Another way to make data first-class research objects is to treat them equally with publications. This has been done through the creation of data journals, in which 'data papers' that thoroughly document the dataset or data collection are submitted and peer reviewed, either before or after deposit (F1000Research is an example of a peer-reviewed data journal, which works with institutional and other data repositories that host the associated dataset). Peer review would seem to be a good way to encourage researchers to make their datasets available and understandable while rewarding them for the extra effort required. Data journals are appearing in a wide range of disciplines.

Reproducibility in science

More is at stake with what one report has called 'the open data imperative' than just a citation advantage for some scientists and scholars. Making data available is critical to maintaining self-correction in science:

> Openness and transparency have formed the bedrock on which the progress of science in the modern era has been based. They have permitted the logic connecting evidence (the data) and the claims derived from it to be scrutinised, and the reproducibility of observations or experiments to be tested, thereby supporting or invalidating those claims. This principle of 'self-correction' has steered science away from the perpetuation of error. However, the current storm of data challenges this vital principle through the sheer complexity of making data available in a form that is readily subject to rigorous scrutiny. Ensuring that data are open, whether or not they are big data, is a vital priority if the integrity and credibility of science and its utility as a reliable means of acquiring knowledge are to be maintained.
>
> (Science International, 2015, 4)

The report goes on to claim, as did an earlier report, *Science as an Open Enterprise*, led by the same committee chair, Geoffrey Boulton, that 'to do otherwise should come to be regarded as scientific malpractice'. This requires that data be made 'intelligently open', meaning that data must be discoverable (through a web search), (digitally) accessible, intelligible (providing enough context to determine relevance) and assessable (to determine the competence of the claim being made and any potential conflicts of interest in a given outcome) (Science International, 2015, 4). Throughout this book, we have attempted to empower data librarians not only with arguments to persuade academics about these concepts on data sharing, but with tools to help them make it easier for their academic colleagues to do so.

Data sharing may be the easiest requirement of reproducibility to meet, even with its known obstacles such as having to write documentation and metadata. Sharing code and models that are re-usable may however be the more difficult task. Victoria Stodden, a computational scientist at the University of Columbia and champion of reproducibility, has critiqued her field for making do with 'breezy demos' rather than making their code available in a form that can be adequately scrutinized. She has attempted to address this inadequacy by creating a tool called RunMyCode (www.runmycode.org) for sharing code and linking it to publications or other claim statements.

Code preservation has not been fully addressed by data repositories, which is a pity since it is one of the key areas data librarians will probably be asked about. The dynamic and changing nature of code makes it difficult to capture in a static form, and its dependencies on other code make it difficult to describe and maintain adequately (though capturing a virtual machine image is one way to try). Code repositories such as GitHub, BitBucket and Sourceforge are useful, as versions of code can easily be identified within a larger body, and re-use is facilitated through creation of 'forks' in existing sources of code, where making alterations is an ongoing process. Another problem with code written for research purposes is that it is often under-documented and less streamlined than code written for commercial purposes, as it is created for a one-off purpose, and often built on by successive postgraduate students. This is sometimes called 'spaghetti code' because of the difficulty in untangling it *(Economist,* 2016). The Software Sustainability Institute at the University of Edinburgh makes recommendations about supporting code written for research purposes, as does the Software Carpentry Foundation, based in Toronto, which runs workshops for researchers worldwide on crafting quality code.

If reproducibility is the new gold standard, achieving it will not be easy. A landmark essay in *PLoS Medicine* explored the argument, 'Why most published research findings are false', including variations in local settings for experiments, low statistical power (based on sample sizes), bias and chasing of P values (which determines a significant finding), at the expense of hypothesis-driven research (Ioannidis, 2005). 'Torture the data and they will confess' is a known aphorism explaining this phenomenon (Achenbach, 2015). A further reason for most published research findings being false, according to Ioannidis, is the sheer volume of scientific papers being produced now, and the competition that engenders.

Some blame the current system of peer review for this sorry state, and advocate changes. Others say that pre-print peer review will never be able to catch all of the false results reported, and that openness is the way forward:

> Given the depth of analysis required to establish replicability, and the increasing pressure on reviewers because of the dramatic rise in the rate of publication, it is unsurprising that peer review fails in this regard. Under these circumstances, it is crucial that data and metadata are concurrently published in an intelligently open form so that it is also accessible to 'post-publication' peer review, whereby the world decides the importance and place of a piece of research.
> (Science International, 2015, 4)

The implication of this is that data repositories need to become more user-friendly, preferably enabling exploration of the data online to save the time of the user and entice re-use and testing of claims made in the literature. Enabling direct links from datasets to relevant papers is as important as making the dataset itself citable through provision of a landing page and persistent identifier. Increasingly, machine-friendliness is another important factor. A new framework has emerged that declares data repositories should adhere to FAIR principles: be findable, accessible, interoperable and re-usable. 'Distinct from peer initiatives that focus on the human scholar, the FAIR principles put specific emphasis on enhancing the ability of machines to automatically find and use the data, in addition to supporting its reuse by individuals' (Wilkinson et al., 2016). For more information about applying FAIR principles to data repositories, see Chapter 7.

Reproducibility, replication, re-use: what is the difference? Computational scientist Carol Goble indicates there are several layers of reproducibility, and there are not three Rs, but actually five Rs, and if pressed she can even list seven! Figure 10.1 shows five of these in a continuum from rerunning an experiment to reproducing variations on an experiment in a different lab. She argues that repeatability is about sameness (same result, same lab, same experiment) where reproducibility is about similarity, achieving a similar result under different conditions.

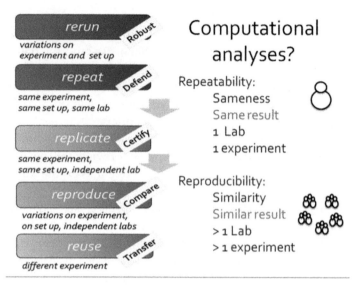

Figure 10.1 *Reproducibility*
© Carol Goble, University of Manchester, 2016. Used with permission.

Do libraries need a reboot?

It is unclear whether academic libraries are responding to the extent needed to these challenges, changes and demands for support in science and scholarship. A number of recent reports have highlighted the need for libraries to get involved with data, and have usefully indicated what types of skills librarians can bring to the equation. Certainly data librarians, where such posts are afforded, can help academic libraries get closer to the research process.

Traditionally, data librarians have not all come from the field of librarianship (nor are they all called data librarians), which makes characterizing them tricky, as touched on in Chapter 1 in discussion of the accidental data librarian phenomenon. But the mix of skills, knowledge and ability brought by members of the profession – many of whom have higher degrees outside library and information science – has undoubtedly enriched the profession, even while making it difficult to characterize. An attempt to capture the career identities of its members by IASSIST in 2008, as part of a survey to inform its strategic planning, is shown in Figure 10.2. As indicated, only about half the membership identified as librarians, with data manager, researcher and archivist being the next most selected identity.

Given this diversity, how can we understand what data librarians and other data professionals actually do? In an analysis of job descriptions from the IASSIST jobs repository over an eight-year period (www.iassistdata.org/resources/jobs/all), researchers found that employers who posted job

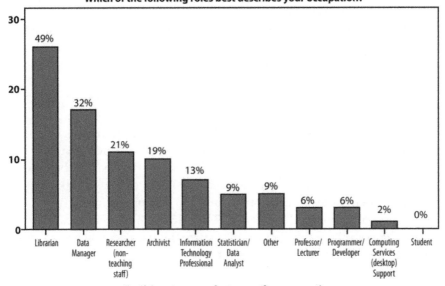

Figure 10.2 *Career identities of IASSIST members, 2008*
Source: IASSIST (www.fsd.uta.fi/iassist2009/presentations/E1_Strategic_Planning_Survey_Results.pps); graph recreated with permission of Thomas Lindsay.

descriptions to the IASSIST members' private e-mail list (and thus were added to the public jobs repository site) valued non-technical skills as heavily as technical skills, with focus ranging from data discovery and collection to data analysis support and preservation. While job descriptions differed depending on whether a qualified librarian was being sought or not, an increasing requirement of data management planning was found for data librarians (Xia and Wang, 2014).

This chimes roughly with the more idealized view provided by one North American library organization. In 2012, the Association of College and Research Libraries identified data curation as a top trend, perhaps for the first time. A study examining RDM roles for health sciences librarians interpreted the trend as being reliant on the following services [emphases removed from original]:

- information and researcher services (e.g., conducting data interviews and consulting on researchers' DMPs);
- metadata services (e.g., annotating and describing data, creating records for data, linking publications with data sets, etc.);

- reference support services (e.g., finding and citing data);
- educational services (e.g., developing subject guides or websites, teaching data literacy, RDM best practices);
- technical support for data repositories (e.g., ingesting data sets and building digital collections, and assigning persistent identifiers); and
- digital curation services (adding value by preserving data and access to data for the long term).

(Creamer, Martin and Kafel, 2014, 262)

This optimism for libraries embracing this role of data curation is balanced by disturbing indications that the scientific disciplines increasingly view libraries as irrelevant to their work, and librarians often feel too busy with what they are doing now to think about changing direction. Is a wake-up call needed, before libraries lose the opportunity to be a player in this new data-driven world of science and scholarship? In 2013 *Nature Magazine* called for a 'Library Reboot', citing the distraction of current library activities as a barrier to entry to the difficult arena of data curation:

> Around the world, university libraries are racing to reinvent themselves to keep up with rapid transformations in twenty-first-century scholarship. . . . For working scientists, who can now browse scientific literature online without leaving their desks, much of this activity goes unseen. For many, libraries seem to be relics that no longer serve their needs. That could soon change. At Johns Hopkins and many other top universities, libraries are aiming to become more active partners in the research enterprise – altering the way scientists conduct and publish their work. Libraries are looking to assist with all stages of research, by offering guidance and tools for collecting, exploring, visualizing, labelling and sharing data.

(Monastersky, 2013, 430)

The *Nature* article also emphasized that changes in publishing centred on open data are new not only for librarians but also for researchers. We would suggest that the key to success in providing modern research support may be in thinking of researchers as partners and collaborators, and in getting them to view us in the same manner. In this way we exit our cosy comfort zones in a spirit of entrepreneurship and adventure, offering not just our existing knowledge but also a willingness to learn new things and tap into an expanding network of knowledgeable peers. If academia can change, surely librarianship can too.

Key take-away points

➤ The open access movement for publications is one of the drivers for data sharing.
➤ California culture of the 1970s and 1980s has been embedded into the internet as we know it in numerous ways; Richard Stallman's GNU Manifesto of 1985 was a watershed moment for open sharing culture.
➤ Big data is a useful concept when applied to new computing challenges, but once the challenges are resolved the term loses its significance, regardless of size of datasets.
➤ Sharing data is not enough; they must be made 'intelligently open' (discoverable, accessible, intelligible and assessable).
➤ Repeatability is about sameness (same result, same lab, same experiment) where reproducibility is about similarity, achieving a similar result under different conditions.
➤ Given that many of these drivers and culture changes for data sharing are as new to researchers as they are to librarians, it makes sense to proceed in a spirit of partnership.

Reflective questions

1. What does 'free as in speech, not as in beer' mean when applied to software?
2. How is the open access movement for publications affecting data sharing in the short term? Will it be different in the longer term?
3. Should data be a 'first-class research object' or not?
4. If so how can data citation help to achieve data becoming first class?
5. Can data librarianship help academic libraries reposition themselves with respect to research support? For some disciplines or across the board?

References

Achenbach, J. (2015) The New Scientific Revolution: reproducibility at last, *Washington Post*, 27 January, https://www.washingtonpost.com/national/health-science/the-new-scientific-revolution-reproducibility-at-last/2015/01/27/ed5f2076-9546-11e4-927a-4fa2638cd1b0_story.html.

Adams, M. O. (2006) The Origins and Early Years of IASSIST, *IASSIST Quarterly*, **30** (3), 5–14, www.iassistdata.org/sites/default/files/iqvol303adams.pdf.

Angevaare, I. (2009) Taking Care of Digital Collections and Data: 'curation' and organisational choices for research libraries, *LIBER Quarterly: the Journal of European Research Libraries*, **19** (1), 1–12, http://doi.org/10.18352/lq.7948.

Arora, R., Esteva, M. and Trelogan, J. (2014) Leveraging High Performance Computing for Managing Large and Evolving Data Collections, *International Journal of Digital Curation*, **9** (2), 17–27, www.ijdc.net/index.php/ijdc/article/view/9.2.17/366.

Ashley, K. (2012) Research Data and Libraries: who does what, *Insights*, **25** (2), 155–7, http://doi.org/10.1629/2048-7754.25.2.155.

Auckland, M. (2012) Re-skilling for Research: an investigation into the role and skills of subject and liaison librarians required to effectively support the evolving information needs of researchers, *Research Libraries UK*, January, www.rluk.ac.uk/wp-content/uploads/2014/02/RLUK-Re-skilling.pdf.

Bishoff, C. and Johnston, L. (2015) Approaches to Data Sharing: an analysis of NSF data management plans from a large research university, *Journal of Librarianship and Scholarly Communication*, **3** (2), eP1231, http://doi.org/10.7710/2162-3309.1231.

Borgatti, S. P., Mehra, A., Brass, D. J. and Labianca, G. (2009) Network Analysis in the Social Sciences, *Science*, **323** (5916), 13 February, 892–5, http://dx.doi.org/10.1126/science.1165821.

Borgman, C. L. (2009) The Digital Future is Now: a call to action for the humanities, *Digital Humanities Quarterly*, **3** (4), http://digitalhumanities.org/dhq/vol/3/4/000077/000077.html.

Boyko, E. and Watkins, W. (2011) *The Canadian Data Liberation Initiative: an idea worth considering?*, International Household Survey Network, IHSN Working Paper No 006, www.ihsn.org/home/sites/default/files/resources/IHSN-WP006.pdf.

Brannen, J. (2005) Mixing Methods: the entry of qualitative and quantitative approaches into the research process, *International Journal of Social Research Methodology*, **8** (3), 173–84, http://dx.doi.org/10.1080/13645570500154642.

Briney, K. (2015) *Data Management for Researchers*, Pelagic.

Burnhill, P., Mewissen, M. and Wincewicz, R. (2015) Reference Rot in Scholarly Statement: threat and remedy, *UKSG Insights*, **28** (2), http://dx.doi.org/10.1629/uksg.237.

Carroll, M. W. (2015) Sharing Research Data and Intellectual Property Law: a primer, *PLoS Biology*, **13** (8), e1002235, http://dx.doi.org/10.1371/journal.pbio.1002235.

Chopra, A. and Madan, S. (2015) Big Data: a trouble or a real solution?, *International Journal of Computer Science Issues (IJCSI)*, **12** (2), 221–9, http://ijcsi.org/papers/IJCSI-12-2-221-229.pdf.

Christensen-Dalsgaard, B., van den Berg, M., Grim, R., Horstmann, W., Jansen, D., Pollard, T. and Roos, A. (2012) Ten Recommendations for Libraries to Get Started with Research Data Management, LIBER Working Group on e-Science, http://libereurope.eu/wp-content/uploads/The%20research%20data%20group%202012%20v7%20final.pdf.

Cirinnà, C., Fernie, K. and Lunghi, M. (eds) (2013) *Proceedings of Framing the Digital Curation Curriculum Conference*, DigCurV Conference, Florence, 6–7 May, www.digcur-education.org/dut/Bronnen/DigCurV-2013-proceedings.

Collins, E. (2012) The National Data Centres. In Pryor, G. (ed.), *Managing Research Data*, Facet Publishing, 151–72.

Consultative Committee for Space Data Systems (2012) Reference Model for an Open Archival Information System (OAIS), Recommended Practice, Issue 2, International Standards Organisation, www.iso.org/iso/catalogue_detail.htm?csnumber=57284.

Corrall, S. (2012) Roles and Responsibilities: libraries, librarians and data. In Pryor, G. (ed.), *Managing Research Data*, Facet Publishing, 105–34.

Corti, L., Van den Eynden, V., Bishop, L. and Woollard, M. (2014) *Managing and Sharing Research Data: a guide to good practice*, SAGE Publishing.

Coyle, K. (2005) Understanding Metadata and its Purpose, *Journal of Academic Librarianship*, **31** (2), 160–3, www.kcoyle.net/jal-31-2.html, http://dx.doi.org/10.1016/j.acalib.2004.12.010.

Creamer, A. T., Martin, E. R. and Kafel, D. (2014) Research Data Management and the Health Sciences Librarian. In Sandra Wood, M. (ed.), *Health Sciences Librarianship*, Rowman & Littlefield and the Medical Library Association, http://escholarship.umassmed.edu/lib_articles/147.

Davis, H. M. and Cross, W. M. (2015) Using a Data Management Plan Review

Service as a Training Ground for Librarians, *Journal of Librarianship and Scholarly Communication*, **3** (2), eP1243, http://jlsc-pub.org/articles/abstract/10.7710/ 2162-3309.1243/, http://doi.org/10.7710/2162-3309.1243.

DCC (2016) Overview of Funders' Data Policies, Digital Curation Centre, www.dcc.ac.uk/resources/policy-and-legal/overview-funders-data-policies.

Desai, T., Ritchie, F. and Welpton, R. (2016) *Five Safes: designing data access for research*, Working Paper, University of the West of England, http://eprints.uwe.ac.uk/28124.

Dodd, S. A. (1982) *Cataloging Machine-Readable Data Files: an interpretive manual*, American Library Association.

Doorn, P., Dillo, I. and van Horik, R. (2013) Lies, Damned Lies and Research Data: can data sharing prevent data fraud?, *International Journal of Digital Curation*, **8** (1), 229–43, http://dx.doi.org/10.2218/ijdc.v8i1.256.

The Economist (2016) Of More Than Academic Interest: professors' unprofessional programs have created a new profession, *The Economist*, 26 March, www.economist.com/news/science-and-technology/21695377-professors-unprofessional-programs-have-created-new-profession-more.

EPSRC (2014) *Clarifications of EPSRC Expectations on Research Data Management*, Engineering and Physical Sciences Research Council, www.epsrc.ac.uk/files/ aboutus/standards/clarificationsofexpectationsresearchdatamanagement/.

European Commission (2013) Commission Launches Pilot To Open Up Publicly Funded Research Data, press release, December, http://europa.eu/rapid/press-release_IP-13-1257_en.htm.

Ferguson, A. R., Nielson, J. L., Cragin, M. H., Bandrowski, A. E. and Martone, M. E. (2014) Big Data from Small Data: data-sharing in the 'long tail' of neuroscience, *Nature Neuroscience*, **17** (11), 1442–7, www.nature.com/neuro/journal/v17/n11/full/ nn.3838.html, https://dx.doi.org/10.1038/nn.3838.

Geraci, D., Humphrey, C. and Jacobs, J. (2012) *Data Basics: an introductory text*, http://3stages.org/class/2012/pdf/data_basics_2012.pdf.

Gold, A. (2007) Cyberinfrastructure, Data, and Libraries, Part 2: libraries and the data challenge: roles and actions for libraries, *D-Lib Magazine*, **13** (9/10), www.dlib.org/dlib/september07/gold/09gold-pt2.html.

Goldacre, B. (2015) How to Get All Trials Reported: audit, better data, and individual accountability, *PLoS Med*, **12** (4), e1001821.

Goodman, A., Pepe, A., Blocker, A. W., Borgman, C. L., Cranmer, K., Crosas, M., Di Stefano, R., Gil, Y., Groth, P., Hedstrom, M., Hogg, D. W., Kashyap, V., Mahabal, A., Siemiginowska, A. and Slavkovic, A. (2014) Ten Simple Rules for the Care and Feeding of Scientific Data, *PloS Computational Biology*, 24 April, https://dx.doi.org/10.1371/journal.pcbi.1003542.

Gray, A. S. (2014) Sue A. Dodd's Lasting Influence: libraries, standards, and professional contributions, *IASSIST Quarterly*, **37** (1–4), www.iassistdata.org/sites/default/files/iqvol371_4_gray.pdf.

Green, A., Macdonald, S. and Rice, R. (2009) *Policy-making for Research Data in Repositories: a guide*, Data Information Specialists Committee-UK, version 1.2, May, www.disc-uk.org/docs/guide.pdf.

Guy, M., Donnelly, M. and Molloy, L. (2013) Pinning It Down: towards a practical definition of 'research data' for creative arts institutions, *International Journal of Digital Curation*, **8** (2), 99–110, www.ijdc.net/index.php/ijdc/article/view/8.2.99/320, http://dx.doi.org/10.2218/ijdc.v8i2.275.

Hampton, S. E., Strasser, C. A., Tewksbury, J. J., Gram, W. K., Budden, A. E., Batcheller, A. L., Duke, C. S. and Porter, J. H. (2013) Big Data and the Future of Ecology, *Frontiers in Ecology and the Environment*, **11** (3), 156–62, http://dx.doi.org/10.1890/120103.

Harford, T. (2014) Big Data: are we making a big mistake?, *Significance*, **11** (5), 14–19, http://dx.doi.org/10.1111/j.1740-9713.2014.00778.x.

Heery, R. and Anderson, S. (2005) *Digital Repositories Review*, University of Bath Online Publication Store, http://opus.bath.ac.uk/23566/2/digital-repositories-review-2005.pdf.

Henneken, E. A. and Accomazzi, A. (2011) Linking to Data: effect on citation rates in astronomy, Astronomical Society of the Pacific ASP Conference Series, http://arxiv.org/pdf/1111.3618v1.pdf.

Herndon, J., Edwards, M., Lackie, P., O'Reilly, R. (2010) *Democratizing Data – the IASSIST Strategic Plan for 2010–2014*, International Association for Social Science Information Services and Technology, www.iassistdata.org/documents/1318.

Hey, T. and Trefethen, A. (2003) The Data Deluge: an e-science perspective. In Berman, F., Fox, G. and Hey, T. (eds), *Grid Computing: making the global infrastructure a reality*, John Wiley & Sons, http://dx.doi.org/10.1002/0470867167.ch36.

Hey, T., Tansley, S. and Tolle, K. (eds) (2009) *The Fourth Paradigm: data-intensive scientific discovery*, Microsoft Research.

Higgins, S. (2007) What Are Metadata Standards, Digital Curation Centre, www.dcc.ac.uk/resources/briefing-papers/standards-watch-papers/what-are-metadata-standards.

Horton, L. and DCC (2016) Overview of UK Institution RDM Policies, Digital Curation Centre, www.dcc.ac.uk/resources/policy-and-legal/institutional-data-policies.

Humphrey, C. (2015) Discovering a Profession: the accidental data librarian, blog post, IASSIST, www.iassistdata.org/blog/discovering-profession-accidental-data-librarian.

IFLA (2001) Guidelines for a Collection Development Policy Using the Conspectus Model, IFLA Section on Acquisition and Collection Development, International Federation of Library Associations and Institutions, www.ifla.org/publications/guidelines-for-a-collection-development-policy-using-the-conspectus-model.

Ioannidis, J. P. A. (2005) Why Most Published Research Findings Are False, *PLoS*

Med, **2** (8), e124, http://dx.doi.org/10.1371/journal.pmed.0020124.

Jones, J. S. and Goldring, J. E. (2015) 'I'm Not a Quants Person': key strategies in building competence and confidence in staff who teach quantitative research methods, *International Journal of Social Research Methodology*, **18** (5), 479–94, www.tandfonline.com/doi/abs/10.1080/13645579.2015.1062623, http://dx.doi.org/10.1080/13645579.2015.1062623.

Karstens, K. (2012) Is the Fourth Paradigm Really New?, *Earth & Mind: The Blog*, 20 October, http://serc.carleton.edu/earthandmind/posts/4thpardigm.html.

Kruse, F. and Thestrup, J. B. (2014) Research Libraries' New Role in Research Data Management: current trends and visions in Denmark, *LIBER Quarterly: the Journal of European Research Libraries*, **23** (4), 310–33, https://www.liberquarterly.eu/articles/10.18352/lq.9173/, http://doi.org/10.18352/lq.9173.

Laney, D. (2001) *3-D Data Management: controlling data volume, velocity and variety*, META Group, Technical Report, http://blogs.gartner.com/doug-laney/files/2012/01/ad949-3D-Data-Management-Controlling-Data-Volume-Velocity-and-Variety.pdf.

Laney, D. (2012) *Deja-VVVue – others claiming Gartner's construct for big data*, http://blogs.gartner.com/doug-laney/deja-vvvue-others-claiming-gartners-volume-velocity-variety-construct-for-big-data/.

LERU (2013) *LERU Roadmap for Research Data*, LERU advice paper, League of European Research Universities, www.leru.org/files/publications/AP14_LERU_Roadmap_for_Research_data_final.pdf.

Levine, M. (2014) Copyright, Open Data and the Availability–Usability Gap: challenges, opportunities and approaches for libraries. In Ray, J. N. (ed.), *Research Data Management: practical strategies for information professionals*, Purdue University Press.

Little, G. (2012) Managing the Data Deluge, *Journal of Academic Librarianship*, **38** (5), 263–4, http://dx.doi.org/10.1016/j.acalib.2012.07.005.

Lynch, C. A. (2003) Institutional Repositories: essential infrastructure for scholarship in the digital age, *ARL*, **226**, 1–7, www.arl.org/storage/documents/publications/arl-br-226.pdf.

Martone, M. (ed.) (2014) Joint Declaration of Data Citation Principles, Data Citation Synthesis Group, FORCE11: the Future of Research Communications and e-Scholarship, www.force11.org/group/joint-declaration-data-citation-principles-final.

Mohr, A. H., Johnston, L. R. and Lindsay, T. A. (2016) The Data Management Village: collaboration among research support providers in the large academic environment. In Kellam, L. and Thompson, K. (eds), *Databrarianship: the academic data librarian in theory and practice*, Association of College and Research Libraries.

Monastersky, R. (2013) Publishing Frontiers: the library reboot, *Nature*, **495**, 28 March, 430–2, www.nature.com/news/publishing-frontiers-the-library-reboot-1.12664, http://dx.doi.org/10.1038/495430a.

National Institutes of Health (2003) *NIH Data Sharing Policy and Implementation Guidance*, National Institutes of Health, http://grants.nih.gov/grants/policy/data_sharing/data_sharing_guidance.htm.

Pareto, V. (1971) *Manual of Political Economy*, translated by A. S. Schwier, edited by A. S. Schwier and A. N. Page, A. M. Kelley.

Peer, L., Green, A. and Stephenson, E. (2014) Committing to Data Quality Review, *International Journal of Digital Curation*, **9** (1), 263–91, www.ijdc.net/index.php/ijdc/article/view/9.1.263/358, http://dx.doi.org/10.2218/ijdc.v9i1.317.

Pepe, A., Goodman, A., Muench, A., Crosas, M. and Erdmann, C. (2014) How Do Astronomers Share Data? Reliability and persistence of datasets linked in AAS publications and a qualitative study of data practices among US astronomers, *PLoS ONE*, **9** (8), e104798, http://dx.doi.org/10.1371/journal.pone.0104798.

Pienta, A. M., Alter, G. C. and Lyle, J. A. (2010) The Enduring Value of Social Science Research: the use and reuse of primary research data, paper presented at The Organisation, Economics and Policy of Scientific Research Workshop, Torino, Italy, http://hdl.handle.net/2027.42/78307.

Piwowar, H. A. and Vision, T. J. (2013) Data Reuse and the Open Data Citation Advantage, *PeerJ*, **1**, e175, https://doi.org/10.7717/peerj.175.

Rans, J. and Jones, S. (2013) *RDM Strategy: moving from plans to action, DCC RDM Services case studies*, Digital Curation Centre, www.dcc.ac.uk/resources/developing-rdm-services/rdm-strategy-moving-plans-action.

Research Data Strategy Working Group (2011) *Mapping the Data Landscape: report of the 2011 Canadian Research Data Summit*, http://rds-sdr.cisti-icist.nrc-cnrc.gc.ca/obj/doc/2011_data_summit-sommet_donnees/Data_Summit_Report.pdf.

Rice, R. (2000) Providing Local Data Support for Academic Data Libraries, *Data Archive Bulletin*, May, 8–9, http://hdl.handle.net/1842/2505.

Rice, R. and Fairgrieve, J. (2003) An Enquiry into the Use of Numeric Data in Learning and Teaching in UKHE, *Radical Statistics*, **81**, 18–33, www.radstats.org.uk/no081/rice.pdf.

Rockwell, R. C. (2001) Data Archives: international. In Smelser, N. J. and Baltes, P. B. (eds), *International Encyclopaedia of the Social and Behavioural Sciences*, Elsevier, **5**, 3225–30.

Rolando, E., Doty, C., Hagenmaier, W., Valk, A. and Parnham, S. W. (2013) *Institutional Readiness for Data Stewardship: findings and recommendations from the research data assessment*, http://hdl.handle.net/1853/48188.

Roose, K. (2013) Meet the 28-Year-Old Grad Student Who Just Shook the Global Austerity Movement, *New York Magazine*, 18 April, http://nymag.com/daily/intelligencer/2013/04/grad-student-who-shook-global-austerity-movement.html.

Rowe, J. (1999) The Decades of My Life, paper presented by Judith Rowe at IASSIST's 25th anniversary conference banquet in Toronto, 20 May, www.iassistdata.org/conferences/1999/decades.html.

Sallans, A. and Lake, S. (2014) Data Management Assessment and Planning Tools.

In Ray, J. M. (ed.), *Research Data Management: practical strategies for information professionals*, Charleston Insights in Library, Information, and Archival Sciences, Purdue University Press.

Schield, M. (2004) Information Literacy, Statistical Literacy, Data Literacy, *IASSIST Quarterly*, **28** (2/3), 6–11, http://iassistdata.org/sites/default/files/iqvol282_3shields.pdf.

Schmidt, B., Gemeinholzer, B. and Treloar, A. (2016) Open Data in Global Environmental Research: the Belmont Forum's Open Data Survey, *PLoS ONE*, **11** (1), e0146695, http://dx.doi.org/10.1371/journal.pone.0146695.

Schumacher, J. and VandeCreek, D. (2015) Intellectual Capital at Risk: data management practices and data loss by faculty members at five American universities, *International Journal of Digital Curation*, **10** (2), 96–109, www.ijdc.net/index.php/ijdc/article/view/10.2.96, http://dx.doi.org/10.2218/ijdc.v10i2.321.

Science International (2015) *Open Data in a Big Data World: an international accord*, CoDATA and International Council for Science, www.icsu.org/science-international/accord/open-data-in-a-big-data-world-long.

Smyth, M. and Williamson, E. (2004) *Researchers and their 'Subjects': ethics, power, knowledge and consent*, Policy Press at the University of Bristol.

Soehner, C., Steeves, C. and Ward, J. (2010) *E-Science and Data Support Services: a study of ARL member institutions*, Association of Research Libraries, www.arl.org/storage/documents/publications/escience-report-2010.pdf.

Southall, J. (2009) 'Is This Thing Working?': the challenge of digital audio for qualitative research, *Australian Journal of Social Issues*, **4** (3), www.questia.com/library/journal/1G1-222315601/is-this-thing-working-the-challenge-of-digital.

Spiegelhalter, D. (2011) Probability is likely to confuse people, *Wired*, 15 August, www.wired.co.uk/magazine/archive/2011/09/ideas-bank/david-spiegelhalter-probability-is-likely-to-confuse-people.

Statistics Canada (2009) *How to Cite Statistics Canada Products*, Statistics Canada, www.statcan.gc.ca/pub/12-591-x/12-591-x2009001-eng.htm.

Sveinsdottir, T., Wessels, B., Smallwood, R., Linde, P., Kala, V., Tsoukala, V. and Sondervan, J. (2013) *Deliverable D1: stakeholder values and ecosystems*, Policy RECommendations for Open Access to Research Data in Europe (RECODE) project, http://recodeproject.eu/wp-content/uploads/2013/10/RECODE_D1-Stakeholder-values-and-ecosystems_Sept2013.pdf.

Tenopir, C., Dalton, E. D., Allard, S., Frame, M., Pjesivac, I., Birch, B., Pollock, D. and Dorsett, K. (2015) Changes in Data Sharing and Data Reuse Practices and Perceptions among Scientists Worldwide, *PLoS ONE*, **10** (8), e0134826.

Ward, C., Freiman, L., Jones, S., Molloy, L. and Snow, K. (2011) Making Sense: talking data management with researchers, *International Journal of Digital Curation*, **6** (2), 265–73, www.ijdc.net/index.php/ijdc/article/view/197/262.

Westra, B. (2010) Data Services for the Sciences: a needs assessment, *ARIADNE: Web Magazine for Information Professionals*, **64**, 30 July, www.ariadne.ac.uk/issue64/westra/.

Whyte, A. (2015) What Staff Resource is Allocated to Research Data Management Services? Compliance and beyond: responses to DCC's 2015 Institutional RDM Survey, Digital Curation Centre, November, www.dcc.ac.uk/webfm_send/2065.

Whyte, A. and Allard, S. (2014) How to Discover Research Data Management Service Requirements, DCC How-to Guides and Checklists, Digital Curation Centre, www.dcc.ac.uk/resources/how-guides.

Wilkinson, M. D. et al. (2016) The FAIR Guiding Principles for Scientific Data Management and Stewardship, *Scientific Data*, **3**, 160018, www.nature.com/articles/sdata201618, https://dx.doi.org/10.1038/sdata.2016.18.

Williams, M., Hodgkinson, L. and Payne, G. (2004) A Crisis of Number? Some recent evidence from British sociology, *Radical Statistics*, **85**, 40–54, www.radstats.org.uk/no085/Williams85.pdf.

Williams, R., Pryor, G., Bruce, A., Marsden, W. and Macdonald, S. (2009) *Patterns of Information Use and Exchange: case studies of researchers in the life sciences*, Research Information Network and British Library, www.dcc.ac.uk/webfm_send/2098.

Wootson, C. (2015) A Call to Deal with the Data Deluge: researchers debate whether an 'overflow' of data is straining biomedical science, *Nature*, **525** (7570), www.nature.com/news/a-call-to-deal-with-the-data-deluge-1.18386, http://dx.doi.org/10.1038/525429f.

Xia, J. and Wang, M. (2014) Competencies and Responsibilities of Social Science Data Librarians: an analysis of job descriptions, *College & Research Libraries*, **75** (3), 362–88, http://crl.acrl.org/content/75/3/362.short, DOI: 10.5860/crl13-435.

Index

AACR *see* Anglo-American Cataloging Rules (AACR2)
accessibility *see* data access
accountability *see* research fraud
ACRL *see* Association of College and Research Libraries (ACRL)
active data infrastructure 80
active data storage (DataStore) 106
administrative data 6, 21–2, 151
Administrative Data Liaison Service (ADLS), UK 21–2
Administrative Data Research Network (ADRN), UK 22
Adobe 116
Advanced Co-operative Arctic Data and Information Service (ACADIS) 94
aggregate data 41, 43, 44ff.
agreement on restricted data sharing 99–100
ALA *see* American Library Association (ALA)
AllTrials campaign 142
Altmetrics 38
American Library Association (ALA) 5, 9
Anglo-American Cataloging Rules (AACR2) 5, 9
anonymization 90, 129, 131, 141 *see also* de-identification
    audiovisual data 99, 100, 132–3
    geospatial data 131–2
    multimedia data 132
    qualitative data 132–3
    quantitative data 131–2
    techniques 124, 131
    transcribed recordings 99
API *see* application programming interface (API)
application programming interface (API) 104, 118
appropriate use 64–5
ArcGIS 48, 59
archaeological research 91–3, 139
Archaeology Data Service (ADS) 70, 92–3, 139
archiving data 101, 139
Arctic Data Repository 94
Arkivum 106
ARL *see* Association of Research Libraries (ARL)
Arts and Humanities Data Service (AHDS) 70
arts, digital 19, 143, 145, 151
arXiv 96, 104
Association of College and Research Libraries (ACRL) 157
Association of Research Libraries (ARL) 61
astronomy data 31, 153
astronomy research 96, 139–40
ATLAS project 140
audiovisual media 20 *see also* anonymization, audiovisual data
Australian National Data Service (ANDS) 75

backing up data 46–8, 115
Bad Science (web site) 45
Ball, Alex 99
Bankscope 60
Bermuda Principles 142
big data 20, 27ff., 150–2, 159
bit rot 115, 119
bit stream preservation 92, 103
BitBucket 154
Bloomberg Professional 59
Bodleian Data Library (University of Oxford) 60, 64–5, 81
    Bodley Oath 64–5
Borgman, Christine 151–2
Boulton, Geoffrey 154
Brand, Stewart 147
breach of confidentiality *see* confidentiality breach
British Atmospheric Data Centre 104
British Crime Survey 7
British Election Study 4
British Household Panel Survey 7
Bureau van Dijk 60
business data 126

California Digital Library 92, 102
Canadian Election Surveys 40
CAQDAS *see* Computer assisted qualitative data analysis software (CAQDAS)
Cataloging Machine-readable Data Files: an interpretive manual 9
cataloguing data files 5, 8–9, 59, 65
CD-ROMs 115
census of population 4
Central Archive for Empirical Social Research (University of Cologne) 7
Centre for Virus Research (University of Glasgow) 95–6
CERN *see* European Organization for Nuclear Research (CERN)
CESSDA *see* Council of European Social Science Data Archives (CESSDA)
Checking a New Item Submission to DataShare 113–14
Checklist for Deposit 113–14
checklist for repository administrators 113–14
checksums 115
Chemistry: handbooks, tables and reference data (University of Oregon Libraries) 38
citation rates 30, 36, 153
citing data 32, 48, 107
citizen science 140, 143, 145
CKAN *see* Comprehensive Kerbal Archive Network (CKAN) 105

Climategate 71
clinical trials 89–90, 142, 145
closed access 111, 139
cloud services 80, 106, 108, 129–30, 150
CODATA *see* Committee on Data for Science & Technology (CODATA) 51
code *see* software
Code of Practice for Research (UK Research Integrity Office) 71
codebooks *see* data documentation
Collaborative Assessment of Research Data Infrastructure and Objectives (CARDIO) 74–5
collection development 2, 16, 22, 53, 66
collection policy 53
Colquhoun, David 45
Columbia University 96
commercial archival solutions 119
commercial use of data 123, 148
commercially sensitive data 124, 141
Committee on Data for Science & Technology (CODATA) 51
Committing to Data Quality Review 114
Comprehensive Kerbal Archive Network (CKAN) 105
Computer assisted qualitative data analysis software (CAQDAS) 2
confidential data 23, 121, 126, 129, 133 *see also* sensitive data
confidentiality 91–3, 124, 125
confidentiality breach 68, 125, 135
consent forms 90, 99, 125–8, 130, 135
Consultative Committee for Space Data Systems, 2012 117
content drift 37 *see also* link rot
contingency planning for data care and safekeeping 97
continuing education in data skills 52
continuity of access 114
Converis 105
copyleft 150
copyright 23, 47, 91–3, 100, 148, 150
Cornell University 105
Cotsen Institute of Archaeology 92
Council of European Social Science Data Archives (CESSDA) 6–7
COUNTER 83
Creative Commons licence 111, 150
Crewe, Ivor 8
CRIS *see* current research information systems (CRIS)
Criteria for Trustworthy Digital Archives (DIN 31644) 117
cross-disciplinary research 38, 123
Crossref DOIs 109
crowd-sourcing 140
crystallography data 142
cultural heritage objects 144
curation *see* data curation
current research information systems (CRIS) 104, 105

DAF *see* Data Asset Framework (DAF)
DANS *see* Data Archiving and Networked Services (DANS)
dark archives 103
dark data 28, 143
data
acquisition 53–5
analysis *see* statistical analysis
assets 55, 72, 74, 84, 98, 143
audit 71–2, 98
centre 2, 7–8, 10–11, 35, 70, 94, 104, 107, 143
champions 73
cleaning 27, 50, 51
collection 54ff., 157
creators 8, 26, 30, 32, 36, 44, 104, 108–11, 118, 123, 134, 138, 152
delivery 9–10
deluge 58, 150
deposit process 94
destruction 123, 130
discovery 8, 25, 29, 35ff., 38ff., 51, 59–60, 78, 84, 94, 108, 113, 154, 157
formats 20ff., 48, 96
from competing vendors 62
gravity 150
handling 50
hoarding 127, 142
in obsolete formats 62
journals 153
licensing 48–9
lifecycle 31, 71, 76–7, 78, 79, 80, 84, 87
literacy 35ff., 43, 44ff., 51
manipulation 16, 50
migration 50, 98, 116, 119
needs assessment 61
ownership 23, 127, 142
papers 153
preservation 8, 14, 23, 27, 31, 48–9, 50, 122, 144, 145, 157
producer 117
reference 39–40, 41–4, 52, 56, 61, 66
replicability 4
retention 130
re-use 29–30, 35, 77–8, 97, 122–3, 127, 131, 138–9, 147, 155–6
revolution 147, 151
science 51, 147
security 47
silo 117
storage 46, 47, 72, 78, 128–9, 130
suppliers changing dissemination methods 62
synchronization methods 90
types 35, 52, 83, 122
visualization 27, 45, 46
data access 9ff., 31, 35, 48–9, 54, 60, 66, 90, 104, 108, 122–3, 142, 148, 154–5 *see also* restricted data access; conditions 111, 119
Data and Program Library Service (DPLS), University of Wisconsin, Madison 11–12
Data and statistics for the social sciences (University of Oxford) 38
Data and Statistics (LSE Library) 59
Data and Visualization Service (Duke University) 12
data archive 3, 6–8, 9, 10, 12, 14–15, 31–2, 88, 103, 107, 111, 114, 131, 138, 150 *see also* data library, data centre
Data Archiving and Networked Services (DANS) 138–9
Data Asset Framework (DAF) 72, 74–5, 98, 100
Data Audit Framework (DAF) Implementation Pilot Project 72
Data Basics 54

INDEX 171

Data Carpentry workshop 50–1
data citation 29–31, 32, 36–8, 51, 97, 108, 113, 152, 155
    Data Citation Index (Thomson Reuters) 37, 118
    Data Citation Principles (FORCE11) 29
data consumer *see* data user
data curation xi, 2, 13–14, 31–2, 49, 51, 57, 71, 72, 80, 83, 93–4, 97, 103, 112–13, 119, 129, 143–4, 157–8 *see also* data management
    Data Curation Profiles (DCP) 75, 92–3, 100
data documentation 8, 25ff., 47–8, 50, 97–8, 112–13
    Data Documentation Initiative (DDI) 26, 108
Data FAIRport Initiative 118
Data Information Specialists Committee (DISK-UK) DataShare project *see* DISC-UK DataShare project 107
Data Liberation Initiative (DLI) 6, 13
data librarian 12–13, 19, 25, 28ff., 31–2, 35, 51, 114, 156–7
data librarianship xi, 1, 12, 16–17, 147–8
data libraries 3, 4ff., 6, 73–4
Data Library & Consultancy (University of Edinburgh) 80
data loss 62, 123, 126, 130 *see also* weeding data collections
data management 23, 29, 32, 35, 57ff., 80, 101
    champions 96–7
    data management plan (DMP) 47, 48–9, 52, 84, 87–8, 91–3, 99, 101, 102, 127, 157
    training programme 48–9
Data Management Rollout at Oxford (DaMaRO) Project 81
Data Management Service (University of Glasgow) 95–6
Data Observation Network for Earth (DataONE) 49, 75, 143
data on human subjects *see* sensitive data
    legal requirements 48
data protection 48–9, 99, 128 *see also* sensitive data legislation 79, 89, 130, 141
data repository 78, 103ff., 106, 107–8, 111, 117, 155 *see also* data centre, data archive, data library
    registry 118
Data Seal of Approval (DSA) 116–17
data services 10, 17, 39, 82, 157 *see also* data centres, data archives, data libraries, data repositories
data sharing 4, 31, 47, 48–9, 84, 91–3, 96, 107, 128, 131, 147, 152, 154
    arts 143–4
    environmental sciences 142–3
    humanities 143–4
    medical sciences 139–40, 141–2
    sciences 139–41, 142
    social sciences 138–9
data stewardship *see* data curation
data user 2, 24, 65, 113, 114, 117, 134
Database Directive (1996) (European Union) 24
database migration 98 *see also* data migration
Database Right
    Australia 24
    European Union 24
database subscriptions 54–6
DataCite 29–30, 104, 109, 110, 118
    DataCite 4.0 110–11
DataONE *see* Data Observation Network for Earth (DataONE)
DataShare (University of Edinburgh) 106

data-sharing platforms 96
Datastream 59
DataSync 106
DataVault (long term storage) service 106
Dataverse 105, 108
DCC *see* Digital Curation Centre (DCC)
DCC Institutional RDM Survey 2015 67
DCMI metadata terms *see* Dublin Core Metadata Initiative (DCMI) metadata terms
DCP *see* Data Curation Profiles (DCP)
DCP Lite 75
DC's Improbable Science 45
DDI *see* Data Documentation Initiatiive (DDI)
deep web 36, 144
de-identification 90, 126, 131–2 *see also* anonymization
departmental repository 107
depositor agreement 116
design layouts 23
DigCurV 13
digital
    bricolage 99
    curation services 158
    data 1, 20, 48
    humanities 144, 151
    preservation 91–3, 114–15
    repository 70, 103, 107
    scholarship 16
    security techniques 90
    'stewards' 114
    surrogate 143
Digital Archaeological Record (tDAR) 92–3
Digital Curation Centre (DCC) 26, 72, 73, 74–5, 88, 98, 99
Digital Object Identifier (DOI) 29ff., 37, 109, 110, 117
Digital Science 105
digital video disc (DVD) *see* off-line storage media
digitized collections 92, 151
    corpora 151
    cultural heritage objects 151
    performing arts 151
    photography 151
disciplinary repository 107
discoverability *see* data discovery
DISC-UK DataShare project 107
distance learning *see* online courses
Distributed Data Curation Center (D2C2) 75
DIY RDM training kit for librarians 49
DLI *see* Data Liberation Initiative (DLI)
DMP *see* data management plan (DMP)
DMP Assistant 98
DMP review service 95
DMP templates for Master's and undergraduate student theses and dissertations 88
DMP to access one of LSE's data resources 88
DMPonline 88, 95, 102
DMPtool 102
DM-Vitals, (University of Virginia) 75
Dodd, Sue 9
DOI *see* Digital Object Identifiers (DOI)
Donaldson, Mary 95
Donnelly, Anne 75
donor agreement form 92
Dropbox 129
Dryad Digital Repository 105, 107, 143
DSA *see* Data Seal of Approval (DSA)

DSpace 103, 105
Dublin Core 24, 26, 109, 118
    Dublin Core Metadata Initiative (DCMI) metadata terms 109, 110
Duke University Libraries Data and Visualization Service 46
Duracloud 106
Duraspace 105-6
DVD *see* digital video disc (DVD)

ecological data 143
Economic and Social Research Council (ESRC) 3, 70, 71, 88, 100
economics research 138
EDINA 49
Edinburgh DataShare 110, 112, 113
educational services 158
Eikon 59
Ekmekcioglu, Cuna 78
e-learning repositories 104
Elsevier 105
embargo 117, 123, 148
emulation 115-16
encryption 48, 90, 126, 129
EndNote 35
Enduring Value of Social Science Research: the use and reuse of primary research data 152
end-user licence 64
engineering research 97-9
enhanced data 55
enhancing usability 63
ephemeral content 48
EPrints 103, 105
e-Research Centre, Oxford University 26
ESRC *see* Economic and Social Research Council
Essentials 4 Data Support course 49
ethical controls 151
ethics committees 125, 128, 130
European Commission 7, 69-70, 88
European Database Directive *see* Database Directive 96/9
European Organization for Nuclear Research (CERN) 105
European Social Survey 7
Eurostat 41, 63, 134
EU-US Privacy Shield 129
evaluating data 43
evaluation 84
experimental data 138-9
experimental protocols 25
eXtensible Markup Language (XML) 26, 144

F1000Research 153
FAIR (findable, accessible, interoperable and re-usable) principles 70, 118, 155
Fedora 103, 105
Figshare 105
file formats 115-16
file migration issues 98
file naming conventions and access controls 98
financial databases 59
finding aids 38
Finding data portal, University of Edinburgh 38
FITS (Flexible Image Transport System) 96
Five safes of data 134
Flowing Data 46
Focus groups and personal interviews 82

FOI *see* Freedom of information (FOI)
FORCE11 29
format compatibility 115
format migration 115-16
FOSTER (Facilitate Open Science Training for European Research) 49
fourth paradigm 150
fragility of digital material 114
free software movement 149
Freedom of information (FOI) 68, 71, 79
freemium applications 150
freeware 150
Full Fact 45
funder requirements 102
funding
    applications 2, 101
    bodies 131
    data services 14, 76
    obligations 122
    RDM services 14, 76

Galaxy Zoo 140, 145
gap analysis 72, 76-7, 78, 79
GenBank, [European Molecular Biology Laboratory] 107
General Public Licence 149
geological research 93-5
Georgia Institute of Technology 75
Geospatial data 42
Gesellschaft Sozialwissenschaftlicher Infrastruktureinrichtungen 7
GESIS – Leibnitz Institute for the Social Sciences 7, 60
GIs analysis software 42
GitHub 154
GNU Manifesto 149, 159
Goble, Carol 155-6
Gold, Anna 2
gold open access 148
Goldacre, Ben 45
golden copies 106
Google 150
    Google Analytics 58
    Google Scholar 58, 108
governance 84
government data 8, 35, 43, 54, 138
grant-funded research 47
Gray, Jim 150
green open access 148
Growing up in Scotland 42
Growth in a Time of Debt 138

Hackers Conference 147
handle.net system 109
Harford, Tim 151
Harvard University 105, 108
HEALPix (Hierarchical Equal Area isoLatitude Pixelization) 96
health research 89-90, 99-100
help desks 14
Herndon, Thomas 138
Hewlett Packard 105
Hey, Tony 150
Hiberlink project 37
high performance computing 150-1
Horizon 2020 – the EU Framework Programme for Research and Innovation 69, 88

INDEX 173

Horton, Laurence 88
http protocol 118
Human Genome Project 142, 145
humanities, digital 1, 13, 19, 22, 70, 143–4, 145, 151–2
hybrid journals 149
Hydra 105

IASSIST *see* International Association for Social Science Information Systems and Technology (IASSIST)
   jobs repository 14–15, 156–7
IBM SPSS Statistics *see* SPSS (Statistical Package for the Social Sciences)
ICPSR *see* Interuniversity Consortium for Political and Social Research (ICPSR)
   summer school 13, 51
identifying variables 124
impact of data 30, 152
Imperial College London 79
industrial design rights 23
infographics 46
Information Commissioner's Office 71
Information is Beautiful 46
information
   lifecycle 1
   literacy 35ff., 46, 51
   security 71, 90
information technology professionals 46
informed consent agreements 126–8
Informed Consent in Visual Research 126
institutional
   data policy 22, 84
   data repositories 15, 95
   repository 74ff., 78, 94, 104, 106–8, 148
   representative 63–4
   research data management (RDM) policy 73
   review board 128
intellectual property rights (IPR) 16, 23–4, 48, 84, 91–3, 100
Intergovernmental Panel on Climate Change's Data Distribution Centre (IPCC/DDC) 143
International Association for Social Science Information Systems and Technology (IASSIST) 4, 5, 6, 13, 37, 43, 44, 51, 57, 88, 156–7
International bibliography of the social sciences 60
International Council for Harmonisation (ICH) 89
   Good Clinical Practice (ICH-GCP) guideline 89
International Digital Curation Conference (IDCC) 51
international name authority systems 118
international scientific collaboration 142
interoperability 117–18, 119
Interuniversity Consortium for Political and Social Research (ICPSR) 25, 26, 36, 40, 60, 63, 92, 102
interview-based research 126
Invenio 105
IP address restrictions 60
IPR *see* intellectual property rights (IPR)
IRUS-UK 83
Is This Thing Working? The challenge of digital audio for qualitative research 132
ISA-Tools 26
iSchool 13
Isis Innovation (University of Oxford) 124
Islandora 105

ISO (International Standards Organization) 116
ISO 16363 104

Java 105, 116
Jennings, Lizz 99
Jisc Managing Research Data Programme 49
Jiscmail RDM mailing list 88
journals in evolutionary biology 143

Knight, Gareth 89
Knowledge of departmental research interests 54, 61, 66
Kryder's law 10

laboratory notebooks 25
Large Hadron Collider 140
League of European Research Universities (LERU) 83
LEARN project 83–4
LIBER, the Association of European Research Libraries 83
librarians as partners and collaborators 158
library
   academic 1
   functions of 2
   instruction 35
   services 12, 95
   subscriptions to commercial products 148
Library Reboot 158
licensing research materials 2, 84
link rot 29, 31, 37
linked open data 118
Linux operating system 150
literacy 44
London School of Economics and Political Science (LSE) 31, 59, 88–9
London School of Hygiene and Tropical Medicine (LSHTM) 89–90
long tail data 20, 28ff., 138, 143 *see also* small data
longevity of the products of digital humanities 144
longevity of URLs 29
longitudinal studies 42, 138
long-term stability 106
Los Alamos National Research Library 37
Lynch, Clifford 104
Lynda.com 51

macrodata 41
magnetic tapes *see* off-line storage media
managed access *see* secure access, restricted access
Managing and Sharing Research Data 49
MANTRA *see* Research Data MANTRA
Mapping the Data Landscape 21
Massachusetts Institute of Technology Libraries 105
McCandless, David 46
media decay 115
medical research 89, 95–6
Mendeley 35
meta-analyses 141
metadata 8, 24ff., 26, 75, 78–9, 94, 104, 108, 112, 117, 144, 145, 152
   content 26
   formats 26
   guidelines 24, 32
   management 32
   preservation 31
   schemas 84, 108

standards 26, 48, 109, 119
microdata 41, 43, 108, 131
Microsoft Research 150
Microsoft Word 115
Minimum Information About a Microarray Experiment (MIAME) 113
MIT Libraries *see* Massachusetts Institute of Technology Libraries
mixed methods research 4
mobile devices 89–90
Moore's law 10
Mosaic 150
multidisciplinary data 108
multimedia arts 151

national data archives, Europe 6–7
National Diet and Nutrition Survey 7
National Institutes of Health (NIH) 152
national legislation and regulations 130
National Science Foundation (NSF) 93, 152
   Arctic Sciences Section policy 93
Nature 30
Nature Publishing Group policy 30
NERC [data centres] 107
Nesstar 108
NetCDF4 (Scientific Data network Common Data Format) 96
Netscape 150
Neuroscience data 28
New England Collaborative Data Management Curriculum 49
NIH *see* National Institutes of Health (NIH)
non-academic use 123
non-commercial licences 112
non-persistence 110
non-technical skills 157–8
NORC Data Enclave at University of Chicago 134
Norwegian Social Science Data Archive 7
NSF *see* National Science Foundation (NSF)
numeracy 44, 52
numeric data 20, 122
Nurnberger, Amy 96
NVivo 48

OAIS Reference Model 117
observational data 142–3
Office of Research (Columbia University) 96
Office of Research (University of Guelph) 98
Office of Research (University of Oregon) 93
off-line storage media 8, 9–10, 46, 57, 115
online
   courses 35, 49
   storage 10, 115
   training tools 51
ontology 32, 144, 145
open access 94, 111, 149
   'gratis' 112
   'libre' 112
   data portals 55
   movement 69, 103, 147–8, 159
   publication 73, 149
Open Archival Information System (OAIS) 111
Open Archives Initiative Protocol for Metadata Harvesting (OAI-PMH) 118
Open Context 92
open data 153–4, 158, 159
Open Data Survey (Belmont Forum) 137

open file formats 116
open (government) data 150
Open Knowledge 78, 105
Open Research Data Pilot DMP policy 69–70
Open Research Glossary xiii, 147
open source repository platforms 119
open source software 108, 150
ORA-Data 106, 107
Orbis UK 60
ORCID (Open Researcher and Contributor ID) 118
organizing data 47, 48
outreach methods 39
overarching DMP 95
Overview of funders' data policies (DCC) 70
ownership of data 122
Oxford University Innovation 124

panel survey 42
Pareto Principle 4, 63
participant training 100
participatory action research 99
particle physics 140
Particle Physics and Particle Astrophysics Group 140
password protection 129
patents 23, 142
paywalls 148
PDF *see* portable document format (PDF)
peer review 148, 153
performance arts 48, 143
Perl 105
permanent digital identifiers *see* digital object identifiers
permissions to use, retain and share data 99, 100
Perry, Carol 97
persistent identifier (PID) service 118
persistent identifiers 37, 109, 144, 155
personal and sensitive data 89–90, 106
personal computers 10
photographs, copyright 23–4
physical objects 22, 48, 144
physical security methods 90
Pink, Catherine 99
PLoS *see* Public Library of Science (PLoS)
Policy-making for Research Data in Repositories 107
Policy on the Management of Research Data and Records (University of Oxford) 73
Pollock, Rufus 78
portable document format (PDF) 116
positivism 3
post-publication peer review 155
pre-print peer review 155
pre-print server 96
prescription 116
preservation 84, 92, 103, 106, 107, 112, 128–9, 131
principal investigators (PIs) 38, 87
privacy 99, 128, 141
   legislation *see* data protection legislation
process-produced data *see* administrative data
promoting usage 58–9, 63, 66
proprietary information 124
ProQuest 60
Protocol for Metadata Harvesting (OAI-PMH) 118
protocols for describing data assets 98
psychology research 138–9
Public Library of Science (PLoS) 30, 140
publication issues 30, 141, 155

publication repositories 104
publishers 148
publishers' data archives 30
Publishing Frontiers: the library re-boot 158
Purdue University Libraries 75, 92
Pure 105
Python 151

qualitative data 3, 99
qualitative research methods 3, 19–20
quality control at deposit 112
quantitative research methods 3, 19–20 *see also* statistical analysis
questionnaires 24
Quick Guide to Data Citation 37

R (programming language) 14, 48
Ranganathan's Rules 39
RCUK Common Principles on Research Data Policy 70
RDA *see* Research Data Alliance (RDA)
RDF *see* Resource Description Framework (RDF)
RDM *see* research data management (RDM)
RDM and Sharing MOOC 49
RDM Roadmap (University of Edinburgh) 79–80
RDM services in place, DCC 2014 RDM Strategy to Action Survey 83
RDM Strategy: moving from plans to action 74
RDS request tracker 99
Re3Data.org 118, 119
reader services *see* research support services
real time data 20
ReCap 74
RECODE project 140–1
records management 68, 71–2, 73, 74
    policy 71
reducing respondent burden 141
reference interview 42ff.
reference management software 2, 35
Reference Manager 35
reference rot 37
reference support services 158
reflectance transformation imaging 92
refreshing media 115
Registry of Research Data Repositories 104
Reinhart, Carmen 138
remote analysis 111
removable storage media 8, 10, 115
removing data from collections *see* data weeding
repeatability 155–6, 159
replication of research 4, 36, 131, 138, 155–6
repository registries 35, 104
Representational state transfer (REST) 118
reproducibility of research 97, 153–4, 155–6, 159
rerun 155–6
research
    ethics 47, 48, 135
    fraud 68, 69, 131, 139
    funding 2, 69ff., 149
    integrity policy 71
    office 67
    on human subjects 125
    project lifecycle 76–7, 79, 101, 102, 122
    project's aims 101
    skills 35ff.
    support services 1, 2, 14, 73–4, 158
research access application 111

Research Computing Survey 2007 72
research councils 131
    Research Councils UK (RCUK) 70
research data xi, 1, 8, 17, 1, 20, 21–2, 48–9
Research Data Alliance (RDA) 37, 51
research data management (RDM) xii, 19–20, 28, 46ff., 67ff., 79, 81–2, 83, 101, 130, 135, 148, 157
    benchmarking 81, 82–3
    course 21
    infrastructure, institutional 26, 67, 72–3, 76, 79–81, 84, 98
    stakeholders 67–8, 71, 73, 76, 84
    toolkits 74
    training 13, 84, 88
Research Data Management and the Health Sciences Librarian 158
Research Data Management Framework: Capability Maturity Guide (ANDS) 75
Research Data MANTRA 21, 35, 48–50
Research Data Repository (University of Bristol) 113
Research Data Service (University of Bath) 99
Research Data Service (University of Edinburgh) 80
Research Data Strategy Working Group, Canada 21
Research Excellence Framework (REF) 73
Research Infrastructure Self Evaluation (RISE) 74
researcher liaison 61
researcher websites 29
researchers as partners and collaborators 158
Resource Description Framework (RDF) 26, 118, 144
Resources for Digital Curators (DCC) 49
restricted data 63–4, 66, 92, 106, 133, 141
    access 60, 63, 90, 111, 123, 133, 151 *see also* secure access
re-use of datasets *see* data re-use
right of use 23
right to deposit 108
rights agreement *see* donor agreement
Roadmap for Research Data, 2013 83
Robbin, Alice 12
Robbins, Jane 12
rock art 91–3
Rock Art Archive (RAA) 91–3
Rogoff, Kenneth 138
Rokkan, Stein 6
role of library 63–4, 68, 87, 88–9, 106, 151, 156, 158
    in research data management (RDM) 78, 83–4
Roper Center for Public Opinion Research 5, 11, 63
Rosenthal, David 115
Rowe, Judith 4
Royal Statistical Society 151
RunMyCode 154
Ruus, Laine 9

Safe Harbor Privacy Principles 129
    genetic data 122
SAS (Statistical Analysis System) 5
schemas 26
Scheuch, Erwin 6
Schield, Milo 44–5
scholarly communication xi, 137, 147
scholarly publishing 148
School of Data 50
School of Library and Information Studies (SLIS), University of Wisconsin 12
School of Research Data Science 51

Science as an Open Enterprise 154
Science International 154
scientific fraud 139, 154 *see also* research fraud
scientific integrity 139
SDSS *see* Sloan Digital Sky Survey (SDSS)
SDSS Main Galaxy Sample 140
secondary analysis 4, 22, 25, 32, 40
secure access 111–12, 121
secure data storage 135
security measures 90, 126
self-correction 153
semantic web 118
Sending your data into the future 31
sensitive data 41, 48, 89, 106, 121ff., 125, 129–30, 135, 141, 142
   economic or commercial 124
   remote access 129
Severt, Cindy 13
Sloan Digital Sky Survey (SDSS) 140, 145
small data 20, 28
small science practice 139
social media streams 151
social network analysis 151
Social Science Research Council Data Bank *see* UK Data Archive (UKDA)
social sciences 3ff.
   data archives 103
   data preparation guidelines 25
   departments 12
   research 3ff., 88–9, 99–100
social surveys 89
software, backward compatibility 115
Software Carpentry 51, 154
software preservation 80, 154
software support 78
Software Sustainability Institute 154
Sourceforge 154
Space data and Information Transfer Systems: audit and certification of trustworthy digital repositories (ISO 16363:2012) 117
spaghetti code 154
Spiegelhalter, David 44
spinoff companies 124
spreadsheets, copyright 24
SPSS (Statistical Package for the Social Sciences) 5, 14, 48, 115
SQL *see* Structured Query Language (SQL)
Stallman, Richard 149, 159
standardization 144
Stapel Affair 139
Stapel, Diederik 139
statistical analysis 3, 43, 44, 45, 50, 78, 108, 157
   software 2, 5, 14, 40, 108
Statistical Analysis System *see* SAS (Statistical Analysis System)
statistical data *see* numeric data
statistical literacy 3, 43–5, 52
Statistical Literacy website 44–5
Statistical Package for the Social Sciences *see* SPSS
statistical publications 19, 45
Statistics Canada 6, 37, 63, 134
Stephenson, Libbie 91
Stodden, Victoria 154
storage fees 94
storing data 48
structured data 27
Structured Query Language (SQL) 51, 151

study participants 90
subject knowledge of data collections 64
survey data 41, 124, 130
Survey Documentation and Analysis (SDA) 108
survey research 4, 19, 42, 44, 126, 138, 151
Symplectic Elements 105, 106

teaching
   data handling 50
   datasets 52
   materials 63, 140
   research data management (RDM) 46ff., 52 *see also* training for users
   with data 39
technical skills 157–8
technical support for data repositories 158
Ten Recommendations for Libraries to Get Started with Research Data Management 83
ten simple rules for the care and feeding of scientific data 38
text data 20, 35
The WELL 147
Thomson Reuters 105
three Vs of big data 27ff.
time-limited embargoes 111, 123, 133–4
time series data 42
tombstone record 110
Torvald, Linus 150
trace provenance and data versions 118
trade secrets 23
trademarks 23
training
   early career researchers 129
   for users 2, 35–6, 47–8, 51–2, 65, 78, 80, 85, 88–9, 90, 96, 99, 111, 124, 134, 151
   in data management xii, 7, 13, 46, 48–51, 71–2, 81, 99, 130 *see also* online courses, workshops
   resources 49–50
   respondents 100
   sources of 50
transaction level data 20, 27–8, 151
transcription service 127
transparency 153
transporting data 48
Tri-Agency funding agencies' data deposit requirement (Canada) 98
trial database access period 56–7, 66
trusted digital repository 104, 116, 119

UK Arts and Humanities Research Council 70
UK Data Archive (UKDA) 4, 7ff., 26, 30, 36, 40, 43, 64, 70, 102, 107, 126
   summer school 51
UK Data Service (UKDS) 70, 88
   ReShare 88
   secure data laboratory 134
UK Engineering and Physical Sciences Research Council (EPSRC) 70–1
UK e-Science Core Programme 150
UK Medical Research Council (MRC) 95
UK National Centre for Research Methods 126
UK Natural and Environmental Research Council (NERC) 70
UK Office for National Statistics Virtual Microdata Laboratory 134
UK Research Integrity Office (UKRIO) 71